To our wives; Joan, Julia and Sinead

The Authors would like to acknowledge the assistance of the staff at Matt Black Systems for their participation in this amazing story.

We would also like to thank Chris Smith, Dennis Kastner, Shirley Borrett, Tony Corbin and Chris Hood for their assistance in the writing, editing and production of the book.

The first truly self-leading organisation

How Two Pioneers Transformed Productivity

Andrew Holm, Julian Wilson, Peter Thomson
MAGIC SIEVE BOOKS | LONDON

Authors

Andrew Holm
Matt Black Systems
Winchester, UK
andrew@mattblacksystems.com

Peter Thomson
Wisework
Henley-on-Thames, UK
peter@wisework.co.uk

Julian Wilson
Matt Black Systems
Wimborne, UK
julian@mattblacksystems.com

Publisher

Magic Sieve Books
ISBN 978-1-5272-6535-6

TABLE OF CONTENTS

Introduction... 12

    Where it started 15
    Where this book takes up the story 16

Chapter 1 - Matt Black in crisis 18

    Background 19
    Passing the buck 19
    Breaking down barriers 21
    Need for change 21
    Design approach 22
    Summary 24

Chapter 2 - Resistance to change..26

    Fixed habits... 27
    Failed programs.. 27
    Outside help 28
    Resistance to change... 29
    Resistance grows.. 29
    Progress thwarted... 30
    New teams versus old... 30
    Keep on trying... 31
    A temporary fix.. 32
    The problem still remained 32
    Summary 33

Chapter 3 - A wild experiment...36

    Crunch time 37
    Buying some thinking space 38
    Tackling the resistance 38
    Changing a rule 39
    Positive results... 40
    Changing a structure 40
    Forcing the change.. 41
    Changing behaviour... 42
    Summary 42

Chapter 4 - Dismantling the barriers **44**

How silos come about.. 45

Breaking down the barriers 47

Purchasing & stock control 48

Unexpected benefits.. 50

Contract metrics 52

New value-added bonus scheme 52

Problems to resolve 52

Summary 53

Chapter 5 - Designing the internal market...........................**54**

Initial growth of an organisation.................................... 55

Design of the organisation.. 56

Creating a decentralised scalable model 56

The internal market 57

From cost to price... 58

Introducing a rudimentary P&L Account 60

Reducing overheads... 60

Summary 61

Chapter 6 - Further decentralisation......................................**62**

The old and the new side by side 63

The remaining bottlenecks were addressed 64

A tight rein on operations 64

Dividing the fixed costs.. 66

Better but not good enough.. 66

A new success bonus 67

Summary 68

Chapter 7 - Making it right..**70**

Maintaining quality control... 71

An innovation in the Lean projects................................. 72

Introducing an overarching philosophy 74

Requirements: Say-Do-Prove 75

Implementation of this singular approach 76

Summary 77

Chapter 8 - Devolving bureaucracy **78**

The final leap into decentralisation 79

Designing a cell admin system 79

A methodical approach 81

Roll out 82

The impact on the cells 82

Summary 83

Chapter 9 - Recipes for succes **84**

Sorting out poor performance 85

Addressing the shortfalls revealed by audit 86

Dividing up the work 87

Managing poor performance 88

Summary 90

Chapter 10 - Leaving the building **92**

Progressing well 93

Further division into cells of one 94

Dividing a good cell 94

Integrating the big picture 95

Conceiving the cells as virtual companies 95

Contract Measures 96

Revealed by the measures 97

Self-management v Self-leadership 98

Introducing the Balance Sheet 98

Transformation to bottom-up 99

Summary 100

Chapter 11 - Power to the edge **102**

Devolving power to individuals 103

Defining the talent 103

Recovering from the fire 105

Impact on business results 106

The 'Fractal' model 106

Freedom within a framework 107

Summary 108

Chapter 12 - Workforce impacts 110

How things were 111

The seeds of change. 112

Picking up the pace of change 113

Playing the new game 115

Surviving the change 117

Finding the right people 118

Summary 119

Chapter 13 - From traffic lights to roundabouts 120

Management Styles 121

Roundabouts versus traffic lights 121

Responsible Autonomy 122

Responsibility to the edge 124

Autonomy to the edge 125

Accountability to the edge 127

Financial rewards 128

Chapter 14 - Payoffs delivered 132

Payoffs from the changes 133

Business benefits 133

Investor benefits 135

Customer benefits 135

Supplier benefits 136

Employee benefits 137

Benefits to wider society 139

Summary 139

Chapter 15 - 500% 140

A quick recap 141

Defining productivity 141

Redesign of admin 142

Reduction in errors 143

Waste Reduction 144

Overcoming constraints 145

Facing the customer 146

Alignment 146

Bringing the parts together 147

Summary 147

Chapter 16 - Lessons learnt **150**

The fractal model 151

Mimicking supply chains 152

Bottom-up versus top-down 154

Differing approaches 155

The turnaround challenge 156

Something to look out for 157

The future 158

Index **160**

Author Biographies 172

INTRODUCTION

by Peter Thomson

For many years, I've been fascinated by organisations that have challenged conventional thinking and proved there are different ways to organise work. When I was Director of the Future Work Forum at Henley Business School, we looked at many examples of employers attempting to empower their workforce, with varied success. There are a few that are regularly used as examples of new ways of working; W L Gore, Semco, Morning Star, Buurtzorg and others. They all successfully devolved power to teams of people to make decisions, and minimised management interference. But none have gone as far as Matt Black Systems.

When I heard about a small company where employees had full responsibility for running the business, I was fascinated and wanted to find out more. I met Andrew Holm and Julian Wilson to hear about their radically different approach to work. We agreed that their changes at Matt Black Systems should be told in a book sharing their experience. It took four years of discussion to unravel their story of turning their ailing company into a productive and successful enterprise. The result is this fascinating account of that journey.

Their problems were typical of many companies, but their solution was radically different. Andrew and Julian challenged conventional thinking and used their design skills to create an organisation that confronted the problems. They were brave enough to try new ideas and let go of control, when most business owners would be 'pulling in the reins'. The company is now highly successful and shows how self-leadership by employees really does work.

Matt Black Systems is part of the aerospace industry. The organisation was, and is, complex. It is governed by detailed standards and regulations. Before telling their story, here's a simplified version of the organisational challenges they faced, just to get you thinking.

Pete and Joe started a replacement window business...

They got appointments, visited customers, estimated prices and closed deals. They measured up, made drawings, built the windows, delivered and installed them, and finally collected their payment. They also did their own business admin. On average, they managed two projects per week, about six-teen windows in all. So, their overall productivity was eight windows per week per person. They were successful and their business flourished.

Over time their business expanded and they hired a bookkeeper to do the admin. Then they hired a sales person to generate the orders, workshop staff to make more windows and installers to fit them.

Their business continued to grow and made money, but life didn't get better. More people brought more problems. Although Pete and Joe had worked well to coordinate their efforts, the new team seemed to find it impossible to work harmoniously. Pete and Joe set standards and introduced more supervision.

Eventually, the business grew to 30 people; averaging 15 jobs a week and installing around 120 windows. This was more windows than Pete and Joe had produced on their own. But everyone seemed stressed and Joe and Pete felt the business was more hassle than it was worth.

They realised that although the company had grown to 30 people, 15 times more than when they started, they weren't supplying 15 times more windows. If productivity had been similar to the old days, their crew of 30 people should be working on 30 jobs, making 240 windows a week. But they only

managed 120. The company had become half as productive as Pete and Joe on their own. Also, it was difficult and stressful. They had done the right things, pursued economies of scale through specialisation, but had become less productive.

Originally, they spent no more than two hours a week doing admin. Now the bookkeeper spent 40hrs a week on paperwork and the salesman and the workshop all took longer to do their part of the job than Pete and Joe had when they were doing everything.

It became clear that the productive work was being completed faster, but everyone spent more time organising and coordinating their work.

When they had organised themselves, Joe and Pete knew everything that was going on because of their wide-reaching roles. Now, everyone in the organisation was spending more time keeping up with events and coordinating. This was absorbing half of their potential production and the result was still muddled.

Matt Black Systems is not a window company, but like many organisations it faced the same challenges. Instead of accepting this as inevitable, Andrew and Julian set about redesigning their business to avoid the problems that reduce productivity. The result is a highly effective solution.

To stay true to the story as it evolves, sections of this book are in italics. These sections are direct quotes from Andrew, Julian and Staff, recalling events from their perspective. I've added my experience from an outsider's point of view. Together we have written this book to show how a unique organisational model emerged.

The real story begins in 2003, but to give some insight into the context, here's their history up until that point.

Where it started

In 1973 two ex-employees of Flight Refuelling (latterly Cobham plc), based in Wimborne, Dorset, England, set up a new company. They saw an opportunity to address the high cost and serious delays in obtaining the cockpit instruments used to control refuelling equipment. The company, James Wilson (Engravers) Limited, was a partnership between a Mr Wilson and Mr James. Aerospace market demand pulled the company along, and it grew and flourished in this niche sector.

The partners had found corporate life over-constrained by processes and structures which motivated them to go it alone. Paradoxically, they then implemented many of the very same organisational processes and structures. They drew on their experience for solutions to their problems. During the 1970s and '80s the company grew and their products became more sophisticated, in line with the advancement of avionic technology. In 1985 Mr Wilson died and his son Julian entered the business as a technician covering his father's practical role. Julian's inherited technical interest helped to solve the challenges of the new products and technology demanded by customers.

The business was now suffering the same ills as other companies in their sector operating traditional structures. They had inadvertently recreated a mini version of their previous employer. After fifteen years, Mr James retired leaving Julian looking for a new business partner. He searched for someone to help with the necessary reorganisation and found Andrew Holm, who was a turnaround manager for one of their customers.

Julian found working with Andrew easy and rewarding, as they shared a common interest in business and engineering. Andrew had a 'big-corporate' background that was especially important for a business that was struggling to take its next step. Before his turnaround days, Andrew had been in large engineering corporations. His experience included design, project management and as a commercial director with a large multinational. He had significant experience of corporate culture and business systems and this had left him with a deep cynicism.

As his turnaround project drew to a close, they negotiated a deal to make James Wilson (engravers) Ltd Andrew's next project, this time as a partner. This would be more than a simple turnaround. Their ambition was to achieve ground-breaking improvements that could apply to any organisation. To clearly differentiate their new approach, Andrew and Julian re-branded the organisation as Matt Black Systems.

Where this book takes up the story

By 2003 many bad practices had crept into the company. Everyone operated in their own bubble separated from the rest of the company. There was constant friction and tension where different departments met, this caused confusion and delay. There was a 'no-blame' culture and yet when problems occurred 'passing the buck' was commonplace. People justified their particular position by claiming to have indispensable knowledge and ability, building an 'empire' and defending its boundaries.

This picture of an unproductive, muddled organisation is not uncommon. Your own organisation may be similar. Julian and Andrew tried conventional approaches but most didn't work, or only worked temporarily. Eventually they found a direction that worked, it was unconventional and took them into uncharted territory, so they had to progress through experimentation. Matt Black Systems is now a self-leading success story, flourishing in a highly competitive industry. Productivity per employee has grown by more than 500%, quality is excellent and deliveries are on time. Customers are satisfied and employees are engaged.

This book tells how they discovered the nature of their problems and what they did to try to improve their situation. The story is not just of their success, but of how they found the path to get there.

MATT BLACK IN CRISIS

Chapter 1

Background

Many business owners and leaders, faced with overwhelming challenges, choose to patch up, sell up or pack up. If they are close to retirement, they might not suffer too much. They may even manage to get a good payoff before the inevitable disaster hits. Keeping an enterprise afloat when it needs radical transformation takes vision, bravery and determination. This is often too much to contemplate. Julian and Andrew persevered through their difficulties and challenged conventional thinking to develop a unique solution.

Their company, Matt Black Systems, designs and manufactures parts for aircraft, ground vehicles, ships and submarines. Airbus planes contain their parts and if you pilot a fast jet or you offer flying doctor services your instrument panel could be one of theirs. It's a small business but is supplying major companies with critical components. In the Aerospace industry strict quality standards apply and delivery times are critical. Suppliers only survive by meeting the requirements of the major manufacturers.

In 2003 Matt Black Systems was in meltdown. Products were not up to standard, deliveries were delayed and customers were unhappy; the business was failing. They had tried everything. Expensive consultants had addressed the symptoms through the adoption of the latest ideas in Lean Manufacturing and Agile Development. Costs were cut to the bone. Yet poor productivity and delivery delays stubbornly persisted. The company was about to become another casualty within the aerospace industry.

Julian and Andrew too could have taken an early exit. But they were determined not to give up. Instead they chose the difficult path of fundamental reform. Using their practical engineering talents, they experimented with the workings of their company. They established ambitious performance goals and holistic business measures to objectively identify success. They could then observe the impact of their changes on these measures.

Passing the buck

The company had many bad practices. Functions had become isolated and work did not flow. The business had become riddled with unresolved problems and no function was immune. A good example was the lack of inspection of incoming goods. When parts arrived, they were supposed to go through an acceptance inspection. But it was more convenient for the inspector to defer inspection and place the parts straight into store.

If the parts were not up to standard when they were used, the problem passed to the production function. For the inspector and the quality department, this approach worked well.

The quality function met its goal of low supplier returns as the production department frequently reworked the bad parts on site to prevent further project delay. But when a Lean exercise was carried out, mapping the production process, the scale of this rework problem emerged. The suppliers were not receiving timely feedback on the quality of their products, resulting in the additional work. It was clear that the suppliers needed to improve their final inspection to prevent the bad parts from getting through, and Matt Black Systems needed to carry out the necessary acceptance checks.

Neither the suppliers nor the inspector accepted the need for change and their behaviours continued. The process only changed when new suppliers were found, and the inspector retired. People seemed happy to produce bad parts if neither they, nor their department, were impacted. Nobody took responsibility for the impact on the business as a whole.

Everyone operated within the limited boundaries of their role, they stayed firmly within their silo. There was constant friction and tension. People justified their position by claiming to have indispensable knowledge and ability. Building an 'empire' and defending its boundaries was the norm. The organisational structure had encouraged political and bureaucratic skills instead of the sales, design and production skills that customers valued.

This was the case for paint spraying:

> *"Our products needed a very high standard of spray finish as we use paints that cannot be touched-up later. Spraying had to be right first time. The sprayer regarded himself as indispensable and did what he wanted, when he wanted and how he wanted. He expected respect and wanted to be paid handsomely for his work.*
>
> *His colleagues felt that he was holding them to ransom. If they challenged him, he would throw his tools down, turn off the equipment and storm out, halting production. Using this power, he would disrupt the workflow whenever he had a point to make. But things changed when he went on holiday.*
>
> *Whilst he was away his colleagues decided to have a go at spraying. They knew enough to practice and practice, so that by the time the sprayer returned they could do the spraying themselves. He was furious to find others*

spraying and immediately stormed out, but this time he couldn't turn off the equipment. When he returned, he knew he had to compromise.

From then on there were two sprayers and within six months the original sprayer left the company. After that, everyone did their own spraying unless they preferred to pay a colleague to do it for them. This example shows how 'empires' collapsed and we progressed, one skill at a time, towards a multiskilled workforce."

Breaking down barriers

Breaking down traditional functional barriers was important in the evolution of the company. There was strong resistance from a workforce that only understood how to work in a traditional functional and hierarchical structure. Outwardly changes would be supported, yet behaviours didn't change. People would resist change in subtle ways, reverting to their comfort zones wherever possible. Making significant change was an uphill battle, at times it felt like Sisyphus pushing his rock uphill only to have it roll down again.

"Not everyone supported change. For some, and often they were very influential people, the increased focus on competence seemed to produce an increase in political manoeuvring. Perhaps they saw a fixed hierarchy as an opportunity to put themselves in positions of unassailable authority? They seemed driven through insecurity to do this; perhaps they were not secure in their competence? This manipulation created considerable dysfunction. Too often we found that company resources were being directed to influence others and foster dependence and control. This was coercive.

We had to be thoughtful in our approach to change to prevent the creation of such sweet-spots and fixed niches where this sort of dysfunction could take a foothold and thwart our change program."

Need for change

The production process was vulnerable because it divided the operation into a series of discrete steps, like links in a chain. A disruption in any step sent reverberations throughout the chain, resulting in disruption and delay. Normal day-to-day difficulties like illness, holidays, mistakes and miscommunication produced serious disruptions. They all affected the smooth flow of operations and productivity suffered. Each problem cascaded through the operation creating more problems and further disruption.

For this production chain to deliver its promise, everything had to go as planned, which it rarely did. In time, a large backlog of work had built up, meaning virtually everything was late. One of the holistic measures introduced by Andrew and Julian was the percentage of products delivered on time and in full (OTIF). When they started their turnaround, delivery performance was calculated at just 17% OTIF. That meant 83% of products were delivered late. Customers were distressed and frequently sent expediters to 'promote progress'.

Design approach

Change would not happen overnight. It would take years of determined effort and a fresh new perspective. Unlike many business leaders tackling organisational change, Andrew and Julian were prepared to go beyond simply shuffling people around and patching up the problems within the existing organisational structure. They wanted meaningful and sustainable change.

> *"We adopted a simple change model. Step one was a situational analysis, we asked ourselves 'where are we now?' The second step was to clearly define our destination, 'where do we want to get to?'. Step three was to make a plan to answer the question 'how do we get there?' and the final step defined the measures that would indicate success, answering 'how do we know we have got there'? We utilised this approach throughout the program, it really helped to bring structure and rigour without which we could have easily gone around in circles."*

This approach inevitably meant gaining a better understanding of the design of their traditional organisational structure and the wider conditions required for it to operate efficiently and effectively. If required they were prepared to design a completely new organisational structure, one more appropriate for the prevailing conditions.

> *"A pilot flies an aircraft and gets the best out of it. Alongside the pilot is an entire crew doing their part in the operation. But the success of the operation is largely determined by a person hidden behind the scenes: the aircraft designer. The designer created the machine that the pilot, crew and passengers fly in. The performance and ultimate limitations of the airplane were determined on the drawing board by the designer. They are not in the hands of the pilot and crew. For the pilot, crew and passengers, the nature of the airplane is fixed. It is their job to get the best from it.*

This situation was not the same for the pioneers of powered flight, Orville and Wilbur Wright. The intrepid brothers had responsibility and control over both the piloting and airplane design. They learned to fly their plane as best they could and at the same time worked to improve the design of the plane itself. For Orville and Wilbur, the plane and their operation of it were as closely related as they were as brothers.

It is easy to overlook that organisations too have a design and, just like Orville and Wilbur, business leaders are responsible for that design and its successful operation. Leaders often fail to distinguish the design of their organisation from its operations. Fewer still take an active role in shaping it. Most leaders 'fly their plane' as well as they can, without ever questioning its design.

This is especially true if the leader is new to the organisation rather than having crafted it from the beginning. However, even when an organisation is crafted from the start, as was the case of Matt Black Systems, its design is often simply a recreation of the founders' previous experience. The original founders had naturally adopted many of the systems and practices they had become familiar with during their previous employment. Within a decade, Matt Black Systems started to experience the same problems that had plagued their previous employer."

The long-term influence of systems and practices are subtle, yet pervasive. Julian and Andrew consider good design is essential if operational problems are to be avoided. Leaders commonly over emphasise the optimisation and refinement of their current systems. Seldom do they reflect upon the organisation's design and its limitations as the source of their difficulties.

The use of simple optimisation can produce excellent short-term results but it can fail suddenly and painfully if the organisation is pushed beyond its fundamental design limits. Such a lack of insight by a leader can result in catastrophic failure through simple activities such as cost cutting. Failure is inevitable, and can be sudden, when an essential part of a design is inadvertently changed or removed.

"As leaders we need to be more like Orville and Wilbur, maintaining a strong focus on the design of our organisation and less like a modern pilot where the design of the plane is fixed. Improvements in the design of our organisations will be enjoyed by everyone because it impacts everyone."

Like many people running a small business, Julian and Andrew faced the challenge of turning their company around. Unlike others, they focussed on their organisational model. If it could not deliver the required results, they would design a new workable model.

In their search for new ways forward, they read many business books. These provided lots of advice but mainly for 'pilots' on how to fly a 'plane'. These books were really about optimisation, with the assumption that the traditional business model was being used. They struggled to find books that focussed on the design of different business (or organisational) models. Nowhere was the critical issue of organisational design explored, even though recent changes brought about by increased access to knowledge, low cost I.T. and networking, provided new opportunities to connect people in entirely new ways. Most approaches to improvement were focused on automating or patching the traditional, functional and hierarchical approach.

Summary

- Businesses are slow to adapt, often only a crisis shakes them out of their intransigence.

- Rather than address the underlying problems, individual departments are happy to 'pass the buck' and avoid the effort of making things right.

- Departments build their own importance within the organisation and defend their domain.

- Processes involving chains of activities are highly vulnerable. One break or holdup in the chain is amplified as it reverberates throughout the linked activities.

- Conventional approaches to organisational change over-focus on optimisation of current operations and under-focus on their design.

RESISTANCE TO CHANGE

Chapter 2

Fixed habits

Matt Black Systems did not set out to be different. Julian and Andrew just wanted to turn their business around and run a successful operation. By the start of the new millennium the company had been going for 25 years. They had employees who had been around for many of those years. Like most manufacturing companies, a management team supervised functions such as design, manufacturing, quality, accounts and purchasing. By 2003, there was a workforce of 25, entrenched in their roles and not about to change. But the business was performing badly, so a change in their habits was essential if it was to survive.

Many attempts to streamline operations were tried in an effort to bring more order and predictability. Yet deliveries were persistently late and there was a large backlog. Dealing with this would require significant improvement in operating workflow. There was not one bottleneck or constraint, but a large number of interrelationships and interdependencies, that bound low productivity in place.

Failed programs

Improving the efficiency of many parts of the operation like manufacturing, logistics and purchasing was attempted. A focussed program tried to open up specific bottlenecks. These improvement programs, based on constraint theory, were not effective and overall productivity remained stubbornly poor.

Some individual changes were effective. New work instructions, assembly jigs and fixtures, combined with improved workflow management, resulted in improvements in specific areas. With hindsight, these positive results were misleading, but at the time they seemed to predict a resultant increase in productivity.

Yet checking business level measures revealed no actual increase of throughput. Each specific area had improved but this had not resulted in an overall measurable improvement. It was difficult to pinpoint the reason. The engines were roaring, the plane was straining hard, yet the overall speed had shown little increase.

For each improvement there seemed to be an equal escalation in problems that cancelled out the benefits. A more thoughtful approach would be needed for overall change to be achieved.

Outside help

The poor performance felt by customers was so severe that they were willing to contribute to a change program at Matt Black Systems, as part of an industry-wide initiative. One customer enrolled them onto their Lean program to reduce the backlog of deliveries and make cost savings. This initiative included consultants who were expert in Lean Manufacturing and its associated toolkit.

This program was more extensive than the targeted functional programs previously tried. It included wider concepts of value-stream mapping and work-flow optimisation (line-balancing). These broad programs cut across many functions and promised to increase productivity because their focus was on 'flow' rather than the output of individual sections. To Andrew and Julian this approach seemed to address the weakness of their previous projects.

At some cost, the Lean tools were duly trained and deployed. Cross-functional processes were rationalised and workflow balanced. Despite much initial optimism and a far larger budget, this program also failed to deliver sustainable results.

With hindsight, though this program was cross-functional, it didn't actually extend across ALL functions. Many remained untouched and were able to undermine and derail each project. As some functions were improved, others became problematic. As these new problems were resolved, the first functions reverted to dysfunction.

Today, Julian and Andrew are clear that detail changes in complex systems will only be successful if they are properly integrated into the whole. Without holistic integration, the untouched parts of a system apply irresistible corrective pressures, eventually bringing the changed parts back into line. A useful metaphor for this is that organisations have a sort of 'immune system' that corrects parts that are out of alignment or foreign (like new working practices). At the time however, program failure was attributed to a lack of commitment to change and it was concluded an even more ambitious program was needed.

The previous program had given rise to questions about the suitability of the layout of their factories. They decided to consolidate two factories into one large unit and expand the Lean program to include all manufacturing. They hoped this wholesale and comprehensive reorganisation of the workspace would result in significant savings in time and effort. This program represented an enormous commitment and investment, but it seemed the right solution to what had become an intractable problem.

The new factory and Lean cell structure would allow the seamless flow of work. New consultants were engaged for this program and there was no lack of commitment to the change program by Andrew and Julian. Their customers could see that big changes were happening. A new factory was purchased and built, and they moved into the new facility, complete with its cell layout.

In time, operations in the new facility settled but, disappointingly, output also settled at the same rate as before.

Resistance to change

The new cell-based production layout had been met with immediate resistance by the workforce. People didn't believe change was needed and were unhappy that their functional roles were being disrupted. One member of staff told Andrew that neither they nor the 'others' were happy with any of the changes. Andrew explained the nature of the customer distress, the need for change and that customers would not continue to buy products that were not up to standard or delivered on time.

The reaction was blunt. This was a management problem and not something that should concern the 'shop floor' staff. Despite a discussion emphasising the need to retain customers, the staff remained unconvinced. They saw it as their job to 'do just their own bit' and management's job to ensure that when all the bits were put together in a chain, something useful came out.

Resistance grows

Initially the change programs focusing on individual functions were met with disapproval, but the justification for improvement was clear. As the programs became more ambitious and crossed into many different functions, they generated a more coordinated resistance. The workforce questioned each change. Andrew and Julian would immediately try to address every specific concern in good faith. But this would often result in new, and quite unrelated, objections. On reflection, the original point of concern seemed just an attempt to block change. When it proved to be ineffective, the employee representative would just move on to a new objection.

"The eventual block was that nothing in their employment contract made anyone responsible for delivering products to the customers on time. It was therefore considered 'against the law' to ask them to do that. This point was both nonsense and a position we couldn't accept. How could the organisation enter into contracts with customers, in good faith, if, within the company, no one was willing to commit to the agreement? The team quickly consolidated around this position as a way to block change; clearly an effective objection."

Progress thwarted

Reviewing the failed programs, the consultants implied that there was a 'hearts and minds' problem. It was essential that employees believed in the program of change for it to be successful. But the consultants had no solution for this 'hearts and minds' issue. They were at a loss to provide a message that would make a difference, when the staff were already clear about the need for change as a result of the visible customer distress.

Operations were dogged by endless new and unexpected emergencies that undermined the benefits of each program. There were draughts and leaks, faulty equipment, rattles and breakdowns. One area was tidied up and everything it contained was sorted. Yet this apparently resulted in many indispensable things being lost or thrown away.

"Of course, we busied ourselves with these problems. It was as though the melee of little problems was generated to thwart progress, to make change so difficult that it would be abandoned. Yet everyone was able to claim they were fully behind the idea of change. But we noticed that the state of affairs always drifted back to exactly the way it was before a program was introduced. We suspected the situation was being contrived and manipulated. Failure was not random, but neither was it obvious how it was being accomplished. Everyone said the right things and participated in the programs, but the overall benefits to the customer and the company were never achieved."

New teams versus old

It is reasonable to expect some resistance to change, however well it's introduced. Change Management has become a business process in its own right and many consultants sell themselves as 'Change Agents'. But the consultants advising Andrew and Julian expected them to impose a new Lean regime because it was a methodology that had been tried and tested elsewhere.

They hadn't allowed for the natural resistance from the workforce who had a vested interest in maintaining the status quo.

For the workforce, any change was bad unless there were clear benefits to them as individuals. Higher productivity meant they would have to work harder or faster and the result would be less overtime and maybe fewer jobs. To them, their objection was an entirely reasonable position, at least in the short term. Just because some new work process might be good for the company and rescue the business, support from the workers cannot be taken for granted. For the business, customers may be lost and profits reduced. For the workforce the loss of overtime or a single job has a more tangible impact on a real person and on the job security of their colleagues. Resisting change is an understandable response. This is not a 'hearts and minds' issue, it is simple logic.

The teams naturally preferred to stick with the familiar work patterns. They fought against any change, particularly ones threatening 'me, my money or my mates' (the 'three Ms' as it came to be known). Teams can be very clever in resisting change, as Matt Black Systems found. Andrew and Julian could continue with rational arguments to support the change, but these were clearly not working. There was a clash in logic from either perspective. Somehow, they needed to find a way to reconcile the clash of logic.

Keep on trying

In spite of these setbacks, Julian and Andrew were still committed to their ambition to properly resolve the problems. It was clear they needed to change tack. Their present course was still putting sticking plasters on the symptoms and they needed results that benefitted customers.

> "When getting in consultants it is easy to go along with a program because they are experienced and you are not. Early on we were victim to just such a program. The consultants identified an area to improve and a benefit that the improvement would deliver. We were fooled into believing that a 5 minute saving in a process, repeated 20 times a day, equated to a 100 minute saving. Multiplied by the factory's £60 'hourly rate', this equated to £100 per day or £25,000 per year. The program looked like an 'investment' and we went ahead with it.
>
> The projected savings never materialised. The adjacent processes couldn't cope and we just got bottlenecks and stacks of inventory elsewhere.

The program was partly sponsored by our customer, who subsequently demanded a 50% share of the 'saving' the consultants had identified. This meant a price reduction equivalent to £12,500 per year. It felt like we'd been mugged.

The lessons learned were:
- *treat consultants with care*
- *be in charge of the measures used to indicate success*
- *make sure the benefits are real and result in improvements on the bottom line"*

A temporary fix

Problems persisted. The programs had cost a fortune and the customers' patience was wearing thin. Unrelenting, Andrew and Julian still needed to resolve the backlog of work, despite increasing fatigue in the workforce for their change initiatives. There was deadlock, somehow the deadlock had to be broken. Apparently increasing productivity was impossible. So, if productivity was fixed, an increase in staff numbers should resolve the backlog.

They employed temporary labour and additional managers to organise the work and resolve the order backlog. If improving productivity hadn't worked, then surely increasing capacity would. This initiative was less effective than expected. Productivity that, up to now had been stubbornly fixed, suddenly dropped. In spite of new people, the backlog remained. However, there were places in the organisation where productivity did not drop.

Some of the Lean manufacturing cells, populated with these new people, performed significantly better than others. It was thought that new people needed training and time to gain experience before they could reach the productivity of the existing team. However, the measures did not support this. The manufacturing cells with more new people were the ones with the highest productivity, despite their lack of experience. Whilst this effect was clearly identified in the metrics, the improvements in productivity proved temporary and unsustainable.

The problem still remained

Andrew and Julian had realised that though the tools of Lean were good, they hadn't delivered sustainable results to the bottom line. There was clearly another factor involved; one that was capable of thwarting the tools of Lean and the other remedial programs that had been tried.

> *"We realised we had approached our problems as if they were an injury to one part of a body and not a disease affecting the whole body. Treatments can be applied to injuries as they are clear and well defined. This may be difficult, but everyone understands the problem and a treatment can be developed.*
>
> *A disease, by contrast, may produce symptoms in a range of different places and these symptoms may appear like injuries. But they are different. They are the momentary response of a body under some stress. If the underlying problem is not addressed, the body will keep producing new and seemingly unrelated symptoms in response to the disease.*
>
> *Applying this analogy to our business, the separate functions operate like parts of the body. They seem separate and discrete, but at another level they are connected and make up parts of a whole. It was this whole system that had a disease, one that could not be detected at the level of the individual functions. Had we been simply addressing symptoms all this time, without dealing with an underlying disease?"*

Identifying their underlying disease required imagination, intuition and insight to understand the common symptoms. What connected them and what sort of disease could it be? They speculated that they could approach their problems from an opposite perspective. They reasoned that if they could cure the disease, all the symptoms would disappear. But it was not clear what their disease was or even if it was curable.

Summary

- Matt Black Systems, like many businesses, had overcome barriers to its progress using Lean, 'Agile' and similar improvement tools to address discrete problems within functions.

- Despite help from consultants, people were resistant to change at every stage. On the surface this resistance looked like a cultural or 'hearts and minds' problem.

- Improvements in separate functions didn't result in overall productivity increases. Improvements didn't aggregate, they didn't combine and multiply, instead most often undermining each other.

- Manufacturing cells with new people performed better than those with legacy staff but this benefit didn't last.

- The cure to their problems was not to be found in the individual parts but rather the system as a whole. It was critical to find out what disease was causing all their symptoms.

A WILD EXPERIMENT

Chapter 3

Crunch time

Things were getting worse. So many excuses were invented for not doing a good job that Andrew and Julian started to write them down. On a deck in a lakeside bar in Switzerland they collated them. There were 146. These excuses were regularly used to frustrate progress or displace accountability. Nobody was taking responsibility. The blame for failure was easy to pass to someone else.

Change seemed to depend on devolving accountability and responsibility. Too many were not taking ownership of their work, instead blaming someone or something else for poor performance. So far, every attempt at change had been frustrated by a disease opposed to improvement.

Andrew and Julian had trawled through piles of management books. They had spent a fortune on consultants. They had confronted the workforce. They had tried every conventional management practice. But something was frustrating their efforts. Maybe it was time to give up and walk away. The money was spent, the 'cupboard' was bare. All the treatments had made no sustainable difference to the performance of the business. Crunch time had arrived.

> *"It was late Friday and I had to resolve the problem; drift was no longer an option. I went through all the viable strategic and tactical options. We had tried everything and were no further forward in terms of overall business performance. When external or internal management support for each improvement 'tool' was removed, the business reverted back to old behaviours and there was not much I or Julian could do about it.*

> *Julian and I arranged a crisis meeting on Saturday morning. It was crunch time. The choice was simple; close down or do something very different.*

> *But doing something very different meant we had to stop fruitlessly patching our old model. Friday was a sleepless night. How had I got here? I'd done everything 'right'. I tried to imagine what else we could do"*

Faced with their evidence, most rational people would have thrown in the towel. Julian and Andrew, as individuals, might have done the same. Together they egged each other on to find another way to tackle the disease frustrating change. Admitting defeat required one of them to blink!

They trawled through everything that had led to the current situation. They had spent a fortune (20% of one year's revenue) on 'improvement projects' and business performance was no better. After hours of analysis and review they turned to the future. What could they do? They were resolute: they would continue. Determined to solve their problems, they were moving into uncharted waters.

Buying some thinking space

Immediately after the crisis meeting, they focussed on their overdue debtors, cut costs further and arranged a bank loan. This secured breathing space to devise a solution by searching for clues to their disease. Together they took a fresh look at the situation.

The organisation seemed to have an immune system able to reject new practices. Apparently, there were two management teams at work, one formal, the other informal. Although the formal one was nominally driving the business, the other had thwarted every change initiative. It seemed this informal team was more powerful than the formal one. This informal management was certainly a powerful force. Julian and Andrew referred to it as their 'invisible manager'. They reasoned that this management force might hold the secret to successful change. Could their 'invisible manager' be harnessed and directed to support the new business direction?

Tackling the resistance

It was impossible to address this invisible force directly. When change was suggested it was simply blocked. It seemed like a 'hearts and minds' issue, something cultural or psychological, a fear of the unknown. From the start of the turnaround program, Julian and Andrew had anticipated this problem. As leaders they knew it was critical to invest time, effort and money in training and support for each and every change. Yet this hadn't worked, so perhaps it wasn't a 'hearts and minds' issue at all?

Maybe their 'invisible manager' was something different to culture, 'hearts and minds', or the fear of change? Perhaps it was something more practical or physical? The physical environment had been changed by moving factory, into a clean modern facility and by creating manufacturing cells. These practical measures had made little difference to the overall business performance.

It could be considered that all of their change efforts had contained implicit threats to staff numbers, overtime payments and job security. Had the Lean program been successful at increasing productivity, there would be reduced overtime and perhaps redundancies. It seemed that behaviours were being influenced to a considerable degree by the rules of their business model, which contained perverse counter-incentives. The improvements to productivity were seen to have negative consequences for individual employees.

This was a new perspective not previously explored, so Andrew and Julian decided to focus on the underlying model used by their business. Their first challenge was to identify a rule that could be changed and see if changing it would lead to new behaviours.

Changing a rule

Data showed little correlation between hours worked and output produced. It seemed possible that overtime payments were encouraging long work hours without increasing production. Changing the overtime rules might encourage behavioural change and potentially influence productivity. They settled upon an elegant experiment that involved removing the long-standing system of overtime payments. This time they would not reveal to the staff the real purpose of this program.

The new rules would mean that overtime payments would cease, although each staff member would still be paid their previous average overtime pay. There were no other parts to the scheme; no other changes to operations. Indeed, Julian and Andrew made every effort to keep things on a regular footing. As part of the experiment, management and supervisory staff were told that the change was to reduce payroll administration. The message was clear: maintain the status quo. There would be no impact on customers, expected productivity or work practices. It was an administrative change only.

The proposal met with general ambivalence and some hostility. People felt they were losing something, but a six-month trial was eventually agreed. After that time, if either party was dissatisfied with the arrangement, it would revert to the old overtime system.

At the end of the first month there was great interest in whether the payslips would include the expected overtime payment as promised. Once people confirmed they were getting their overtime pay without their hours being tracked, they began to adapt their behaviours.

In the second month something new happened. One member of the production staff increased his work rate so he reached his target at the end of the standard day and didn't need to work overtime as he had done previously. Everyone again paid special attention to his pay-packet that month to confirm that he was paid his 'overtime', even though he no longer worked any extra hours.

Over the next four months, all the staff members changed their behaviour. Everyone went home on time. Actual hours worked fell by 20%, equivalent to previous overtime hours. Yet quality and output remained the same, representing a significant productivity gain.

Positive results

After six months the experiment was evaluated, as promised. By now, everyone worked their minimum contracted hours. Despite the significant drop in hours worked, revenue had not shifted materially. Quality and delivery figures remained the same, if not slightly improved.

This is not what was expected. The stubbornly fixed productivity, combined with fewer working hours, should have reduced revenue and impacted other performance measures. Instead there was a 20% jump in productivity that was stable and sustainable. The changes had been transmitted to the overall business performance and were detected by the top-level measures used by Julian and Andrew. Somehow, a change that cost very little had delivered more in terms of productivity and sustainable performance than all their previous projects.

It was now clear that there was something else influencing performance, something like their 'invisible manager'. What the formal management structure had failed to deliver in years was being delivered by an informal structure, cost free. And when the staff were given the opportunity to return to the previous overtime system, they declined.

Changing a structure

Andrew and Julian decided to make more changes to their ruleset. However, they soon realised that their rules were heavily interdependent. They were part of a web or network with many cross-references just like the rules of a game. They were not individual or isolated. It was difficult to find a rule to change that didn't produce a detrimental impact on the system as a whole. The rules they wanted to change were so deeply interconnected that they couldn't change them. First, they had to make preparatory changes just to free up the rules they wanted to change. It is a challenge to change the rules of any game whilst you are playing it.

Whilst the approach was producing results, Andrew and Julian focussed on reducing the risks of this unconventional experiment. By dividing the organisation into smaller parts any unforeseen problems would be limited to a small part of the organisation rather than affect the whole.

As a result of their previous failed Lean program, they had four customer-facing manufacturing cells. They decided to break up the shared administrative systems and devolve them into the four cells. Although this would duplicate admin activities, it would reduce risk. It would also provide an opportunity to streamline the admin tasks prior to devolution.

Rule changes were being introduced to increase the sense of ownership by the staff. If each manufacturing cell purchased and looked after the stock needed to fulfil their customer contracts, they would have greater ownership. To do this, the old central store had to close and its contents moved to the individual cells.

Julian and Andrew discussed the move with the storemen and the cell teams, who agreed to move the inventory into their manufacturing cells within two weeks. Then the stores staff would integrate into the cell teams. After the agreed two weeks, progress was reviewed. Nothing had changed.

Forcing the change

Julian and Andrew repeated their discussion with the cell teams and agreed another target for closing down the stores. Again, nothing changed. It seemed this change was not going to happen voluntarily so Julian and Andrew decided to do it themselves.

> *"Over one weekend, we emptied the central store, randomly, into the four manufacturing cells. We dismantled the store walls and painted the floor. The central stores area had disappeared leaving no sign it ever existed.*

> *On Monday morning the storemen arrived and stood where the stores had been, exactly in the positions their chairs had occupied. It took most of the morning before the stores people moved to stand in the cells that now contained the randomly distributed inventory. Old habits die hard."*

It took this change to the physical structure to trigger the desired behaviours, and some time for the people to settle into a multiskilled productive role of their own making.

Changing behaviour

Looking back at changing the overtime rules, Andrew and Julian saw that they had learned a valuable lesson. However logical a change may seem to be, behaviours don't change even when people say they are engaged in it. Change had to be triggered by something. Staff were given the option to earn 'overtime' without working overtime hours. This changed the 'logic' of overtime from the perspective of the individual. Behaviours changed; jobs got done without needing to work extra hours. They improved productivity, because it was in their best interest to do so. They gained as individuals.

There were similar learnings from closing down the stores. People agreed to implement the decision but had no commitment to it because the logic was not clear how they would gain as individuals. This time the change had to be triggered by a change in the physical structure. Once the stores were gone, people implemented the plan and changed their behaviour. In each case a catalyst was needed for new behaviours to emerge and evolve.

These experiences helped Andrew and Julian recognise the keys to effective change: shift the physical structure to support new behaviours, change the ruleset, and have top level measures in place to monitor the end results. All in pursuit of a new logic.

Instead of resorting to 'command and control', telling people what to do, now they would redesign the physical structure and the organisational rule-set leaving the invisible manager to align and benefit from their new logic. In this way they would come to accomplish successful change.

Summary

- If sustainable change is elusive then stop repeating the same approach. You are probably treating symptoms. You need to see if there is a hidden disease undermining your programs.

- The rule for overtime was changed, removing the incentive to work long hours. As a result, people stopped working overtime whilst maintaining their output; resulting in a productivity improvement of 20%.

- The informal management team was more powerful and effective than the formal one. It pursued the internal logic of the structure and rule set as if it were the winning strategy of a game.

- The structure of the stores was changed so the old behaviours were no longer supported. As a result, the stores were integrated into the manufacturing cells.

- People in the manufacturing cells were accountable for their own stock; producing an improvement in 'ownership'.

- Julian and Andrew realised that behaviours can be changed by redesign of the ruleset and the removal of physical boundaries that support silo behaviours.

DISMANTLING THE BARRIERS

Chapter 4

How silos come about

During the 20th Century we accepted that organisations were best structured around functions and departments. Sales, Accounts and Production are familiar functions within traditional organisations. As organisations grow, these functions often grow faster and separate into further sub-functions like Marketing, Accounts Receivable and Quality Management.

Typically, when people join an enterprise they enter via a position within a function and build their career from this foundation. It is rare to find an individual with cross-functional experience. Most advance by promoting the interests of their function and inevitably rivalry between functions is common. Language and communication links between functions are often strained as each have different interests, focus and objectives. Tensions between these separate silos is ever present. Effort is required to keep things from deteriorating into outright conflict. This adds to the tendency for functions to grow faster than the organisation as a whole.

It's not just the head count of each department that grows. The operating costs will also grow faster than the wider organisation that it supports. This is the accepted norm and this tendency is embraced as inevitable (see Parkinson's Law below).

Parkinson's Law

Work expands to fill the time available. Cyril Parkinson attributed his 'law' to two underlying forces. Firstly, the desire for the people to increase the number of their subordinates and secondly, the fact that administrators make work for one other. Thus, he observed, bureaucracy grows by 5-7% per year irrespective of the growth of the wider organisation. This observation was made within the context of the traditional functional and hierarchical organisational structure, something that Parkinson himself did not clearly distinguish. What Parkinson was observing was an artefact of the organisational model and not a universal truth.

A simple but revealing test for many organisations is how revenue (value of sales) per employee changes over the years. One might expect this to improve every year as people get better at their jobs and gain greater economy of scale. Most commonly, the revenue per person per year declines and this is accepted without challenge.

Historical example

The Scottish ship building industry was a prime example of this overall decline in productivity. In its prime, the industry was highly successful. During the early part of the 20th century the Clyde built more than 20% of all the ships in the world. The ship building process was highly organised and successful, yet by the 1970s its competitiveness was declining rapidly. New competitors appearing in the Far East became a threat. Although their labour costs were lower, it was their higher productivity that set them apart.

In countries such as South Korea they didn't demark their workforce by skills. Instead packages of work were given to multiskilled teams. This approach simplified coordination of the workforce and therefore required less administrative overhead. In Scotland by contrast, completing a compartment of a ship meant the coordination of many specialists. Specialists were not allowed to practice the skills of other specialists. This was essential to avoid demarcation disputes. This approach required the right specialists, with the right tools, at the right time, to go to the right place to do their job. Despite its complexity this system got compartments built, but wasted a huge amount of time. In addition, the shipyard employed an army of coordinators.

How many Scottish shipbuilders does it take to change a light bulb?
In 1966 it really did take five people to change an overhead light bulb.
Demarcation demanded:
a Labourer (member of the Transport and General Workers Union) to carry the ladder to site, a Rigger (member of the Amalgamated Society of Boilermakers, Shipwrights, Blacksmiths and Structural Workers Union) to erect the ladder in its proper position, an Electrician (member of the Electrical Trades Union) to remove the old bulb and screw in the new one, a Foreman to schedule and co-ordinate the project and check the outcome and finally a Clerk to capture the timesheets and complete the necessary admin.

Reducing costs and improving efficiency became a matter of survival for Scottish shipbuilders, yet demarcation and specialisation meant changes were a threat to the jobs of individual workers.

Management wanted to improve productivity but protect their admin teams. The unions, representing workers, wanted to protect their members' jobs as well as skill demarcation. The organisational model of specialisations and functional silos fostered and fuelled this conflict. Without a change to the model, decline and ultimate demise was inevitable.

The problem facing the Scottish shipbuilding industry was mischaracterised as conflict between management and workforce. But their opposing positions were the result of an organisational model that set the parties in logical conflict rather than in alignment. The conflict would persist as long as the model persisted. Fix the conflict, and the broken logic would still drive the organisation into failure. Fix the logic and the conflict could be resolved and the organisation's competitiveness could improve.

Few, if any, in the industry distinguished the underlying logic problem within their model, nor as individuals did they have the ability to introduce a new model. That would demand a different way of working.

A historical alternative

By contrast in Korea, a multiskilled team, led by an on-the-job engineer, was tasked with the package of work to complete a compartment. There was less movement of workers and a lower coordination burden, for planning, administering and inspecting work. Less movement, less wasted time, less remote managerial burden resulted in increased productivity and lower costs. In addition, it was easy to determine who was responsible for poor quality or delays.

For the Koreans, the model translated into cheaper, higher quality ships. In the competitive world of shipbuilding, Korea used this advantage to grow and become a world player in shipbuilding. In the 12 years between 1980 and 1992 the Korean ship building industry grew from 7% of the global market to 35%. It has dominated ship production ever since. Korean ships were not materially different to Scottish ones, but the organisational model they used was.

Breaking down the barriers

Matt Black Systems, had four Lean work cells with, on average, four people per cell. These were the remnants of their failed Lean program. Whilst the work was devolved into these work cells, their management and administration still took place centrally. Julian and Andrew decided the work cells should pursue the Korean shipbuilding approach.

Their Lean project had tidied these work cells, introduced process standards and driven out waste. The new approach would integrate the associated management and admin processes, even if it resulted in duplication. This would place responsibility on the cells, for satisfying contracts rather than just delivering products. Work cells would have more autonomy, more control, and more decision-making authority.

The leap in productivity from the overtime experiment had shown no further productivity gain once the time reward was maximised. But Julian and Andrew were keen to use what they had learnt to address the order backlog. This time they would offer a financial reward to each cell for working through their backlog of contracts. This backlog caused great distress to their customers, it was hoped this simple financial reward would be just as effective as the time reward at changing behaviour. The extra sales revenue from working off the backlog, in addition to the baseline sales, would increase revenue. A proportion of this projected revenue would pay for this new bonus program.

Discussions about this new bonus were more positive because of the success of the overtime experiment. Whilst the idea was accepted, the work cells decided they needed more control. They wanted control of incoming goods because the late arrival of parts delayed assembly. It was agreed that responsibility for procurement should also be integrated into each cell. This improved the chance of success but meant a disruption to the central purchasing function.

This additional change provided the opportunity to introduce a new performance measure. The value of sales and the value of purchases for each work cell could be utilised to indicate the value-added by the cell through their efforts. For Andrew and Julian this was a key step to reduce the reliance on time as a measure and emphasise instead the value being provided to customers. Purchasing and stock control functions were integrated into each of the four work cells.

> *"This exciting project gave us hope for the future. However, the program created tensions between those in the work cells and those still operating in the centralised functions. It was clear we would have to manage these tensions to give this experiment a fair chance to prove itself. Those who weren't part of it could not be allowed to deliberately undermine it."*

Purchasing & stock control

Each cell would purchase and control its own stock and feel ownership for it. A simple stand-alone purchasing system was designed and introduced into the work cells. The system was more logical and efficient and cut the process cost by 90%. Various reporting and authorisation loops between the accounts, purchasing, stores and production management could be removed as they now occurred within each cell. For the cell, these extra responsibilities were a burden but they willingly undertook them for the promise of extra control and the new 'backlog bonus'.

The new purchasing system was based on the assumption that all aspects of purchasing and stock control were carried out by a single team, who knew all they needed to know. This allowed the redesigned process to be simple because it required so little transfer of information. For the person doing the purchasing, being 'in the know' was the critical factor for simplification. Whilst the number of steps and the costs were reduced, the redesigned purchasing approach also increased the checks and measures within the process. Julian and Andrew were keen to try new ideas, even radical ones, but only if the risks were thoughtfully managed.

"As the purchasing process changed, work cells ordered the parts they needed and incoming inventory passed directly to the work cell, where it was stored. This was seen as a benefit to the overstretched central purchasing and admin team. By contrast, the production manager became increasingly aware that he was losing his grip on the work cells which, in turn, was diminishing his ability to re-prioritise work in the factory overall.

This is an example of the sorts of tensions that grow when different approaches co-exist. They are inevitable during any period of transition. We made an effort to reduce these tensions as they appeared."

There was an assumption that some people in the work cells might resist the devolution of purchasing, but this was unfounded. People were already multiskilled, through the demands of their home life, yet the organisation had never recognised this or placed such an expectation upon them. As the purchasing responsibility was embraced, it became clear that they already had a baseline of untapped experience and did not need to develop these skills from scratch.

Without a central store, new inventory passed directly to the work cells. This required a new and simplified stock control system. The control of procurement and stock by the cell led to a dramatic reduction in the administrative costs and removed the needless delays of components. Although purchasing and stock control was duplicated in each cell, the overall reductions in cost and delay far exceeded the performance of the previously centralised functions. This improvement in logistics resulted in the smoothing of operations. There were fewer interruptions to the work flow and everything was calmer and more predictable.

There was also a positive impact on suppliers.

"The suppliers were held to account more effectively by the work cells than by the centralised teams. The instant feedback on incorrect goods and services meant they were forced to change behaviours. Supplies became much more consistent, in quality and delivery.

From the point of view of suppliers, several buyers now provided them with orders but demands were uncoordinated and often conflicted. For large suppliers this was not a problem because they treated all their orders independently. However, certain smaller suppliers were confused because they were accustomed to a centralised buyer constantly re-ordering their schedules.

These suppliers tended to prioritise projects from the central buyer and delay those received from the work cells.

However, this led to them being deselected by the work cell, as a result of not meeting agreed delivery terms. The smarter suppliers treated different buyers equally and gained as a result. By contrast, the central buyer found their leverage on the suppliers was diminished and saw this as a loss of 'flexibility'. Tensions grew both within the company and with some suppliers. We intervened to give suppliers an overview of the wider company changes and helped the central buyer adapt to their reduction in leverage."

Unexpected benefits

Perhaps the most surprising result of decentralising purchasing and stock control was that the cost of parts dropped. The work cells were clearly capable of managing the purchase administration and of negotiating better prices.

The simplicity of coordinating a decentralised operation had a big payoff. The right parts were ordered at the right time and in the right quantity because they were purchased by the people most familiar with the requirements. On arrival, the parts were properly checked as they were being inspected by the people who were most familiar with them and who were going to utilise them. The price advantage of buying in bulk, the promise of centralised purchasing, proved to be insignificant compared to the many advantages of decentralised purchasing. Indeed, the specific prices paid for individual parts actually fell, probably the result of increased negotiation by the cells.

These counter-intuitive benefits were so significant that they covered the cost of creating the new purchasing and stock control systems within three months. After that, savings showed on the bottom line through a reduction in costs and an increase in productivity.

"The theme was always the same. No system was decentralised without proper redesign to make it fit for purpose. Coordination across multiple centralised admin and management functions was where the bulk of our hidden costs and delays were to be found. Decentralising was an opportunity to remove these costs. Placing the task with someone 'in the know' was the key to simplification and savings.

Within a single work cell, the complexity of each task was reduced to something familiar, easy and straightforward. Yet an individual, in the know, was able to see each task in its wider context, allowing them to strike more sophisticated compromises. In hindsight, it became clear that centralisation is a burden that adds hidden cost and complexity.

We discovered that the original foundation of Lean was not tools like '5S (Sort, Set in order, Shine, Standardise and Sustain)' and '5Whys (root cause analysis)' as we had been led to believe. It was the concept of colocated, work cell teams that was at the heart of the original Japanese programs."

The procurement experiment rested upon the incentive of the backlog bonus. It proved very effective for a while. As the backlog fell, revenue increased more than was paid in cell team bonus. The increase in productivity of the whole company (revenue per person) provided the evidence needed to confirm the success of the project. Productivity grew and profits improved. The increase in profit was greater than the cost increase of the entire program. Better still, customers noticed the reduction in their order backlog and responded positively.

An unexpected benefit to the program was greater engagement of the cell teams. They had a positive attitude and greater confidence and self-esteem from their success. This was readily observable, if difficult to quantify.

This latest change set a vision for the way ahead using the Korean ship building model of decentralisation and multiskilling. The work cells had become multifunctional cells representing the leading edge within Matt Black Systems, whilst the remaining centralised part represented its trailing edge.

With the backlog reducing, some cells worked off their late deliveries completely and as a consequence could no longer earn a backlog bonus. In the rush to earn bonus, some cells cut corners. The unreformed cells carried on working off their backlog and enjoying their backlog bonus. For those cells that had worked off their backlog, what was needed was an objective differentiation between those that had cut corners and those that hadn't.

A system was required, that rewarded the value-added by the cell. But, 'value' includes more than just money. It includes quality, delivery, price and control, all essential properties of a customer contract. It was this wider definition of value-added that was key to a bonus scheme for those cells without a backlog. Capturing these additional contract properties would be the proper way to differentiate the cells that didn't cut corners.

Contract metrics

Research into measurement regimes was fruitless, they were either incorrectly focussed or too complicated. The multifunctional cells needed simple measures that could distinguish how well contracts were being satisfied. A simplified approach was created based on four metrics. These were the synthesis of the contract properties. Every contract has four properties:

- *Quality* describes the characteristics of the outcome being demanded,
- *Delivery* describes when the outcome is required and in what quantity,
- *Price* is simply the agreed price promise,
- *Control* describes the statutory, regulatory and wider constraints that apply.

In addition to the top-level financial measures, these simple contract metrics formed a generic approach to all performance monitoring.

New value-added bonus scheme

Combining the rudimentary financial measures and the new contract metrics paved the way for a new bonus regime. Each cell could achieve a value-added bonus based on both the financial value they added, combined with the successful satisfaction of their contracts. This new bonus provided the necessary fillip to the staff who had been most successful at reducing their backlog and not cutting corners.

Problems to resolve

Having introduced the new metrics regime, Andrew and Julian found that devolving purchasing posed some challenges:

> "There was always a worry about losing control of cash flow, holding excess stock or missing out on economies of scale. One day, soon after devolving purchasing, a large consignment of glue syringes arrived. Someone had ordered 13 years of stock because of a small price advantage when purchased in bulk. To them, it made sense as they were not, at that time, responsible for the capital tied up in the stock."

This experience didn't derail the decentralisation project. It provided further focus on checks and balances to avoid unintended logical consequences. Perverse incentives emerge if operations are not decentralised thoughtfully and thoroughly.

Summary

- In silo organisations, management and admin effort goes into maintaining order within the function and coordinating activities between functions. The hidden cost of internal control and cross-functional coordination is borne by the value adding operations (sales, design & production).

- Matt Black Systems circumvented the centralised purchasing department, devolving the function into the work cells. This decentralised approach removed delays and improved the supply of parts.

- The decentralisation of purchasing and stock control resulted in considerable improvement in the coordination, flow and efficiency of each work cell. Things went more smoothly.

- The small increase in burden for the cell to purchase and control their stock was more than offset by the removal of the larger costs of the centralised functions.

- Introducing a backlog bonus provided an incentive to improve productivity further, and the increase in sales more than covered the cost of the change program.

- With the introduction of purchasing and stock control, the work cells had become multifunctional cells.

DESIGNING THE INTERNAL MARKET

Chapter 5

Initial growth of an organisation

As they grow, most businesses introduce specialisation, subdivide into functions and set up layers of management to coordinate these functions. This traditional scaling method is not the only option. Matt Black Systems has proved that using autonomous multifunctional cells is a viable alternative. So, what makes the traditional approach so prevalent?

A sole trader, finds customers, does the work, delivers the products, deals with suppliers and keeps the accounts. As the business grows something has to change. A bookkeeper records transactions, a sales person wins business and design separates from production. Business functions divide. The owner must evolve processes that enable products and information to flow seamlessly between functions. The processes need coordination, so management and administration functions are added to the specialist functions. A silo organisation results.

Once departments are formed, each one has its own priorities. Sales want bigger orders to increase bonuses. Manufacturing want a regular flow of orders to promote smooth workflow. Finance want to reduce costs to improve profitability. Quality want to increase costs to improve compliance.

At budget time, all the departments fight for their share of a finite 'cake', with limited appreciation of the contribution of other departments. The company and revenue may grow, but profit as a percentage will decline.

Is there another way of growing a business? Is specialisation into functions essential? Could a decentralised cell model work? Julian and Andrew declared a resounding "yes". Decentralised cells keep responsibilities and accountability wide and reward is based on what is produced.

But these are not simple questions with simple answers. Any alternative approach solves certain problems but introduces many others. It is not a question of how to eliminate problems, but which set of problems is best to live with in the long term.

> *"We chose to define the problems we wanted rather than try to create a magical system that had no problems. It was better to have several problems that could be addressed rather than even one insurmountable problem. It's not the number of problems, it's whether they limit the organisation or even threaten its existence. The organisational design you adopt will determine the set of problems you have to live with.*

Organisational design is the most neglected role of the directors. It is their job to choose a manageable set of problems for their organisation. Often the design of the organisation is considered a 'given', its problems unavoidable.

We chose to change our model because the problems we had were threatening our business. We wanted a better set of problems."

Design of the organisation

There is a clear separation in the roles of directors and managers. The role of the management team is *operational*. They 'fly the aeroplane' just like its pilot and crew. The role of the board of directors is to define the organisation. They are the equivalent of the aircraft designer. Most commonly, the directors become embroiled in operational and management concerns and neglect their role as organisational designers. This is perhaps inevitable when each director leads a department and only at board level do departments become a team. Whilst they should be focussed **on** the business, all too often they deal with issues **in** the business.

Without sufficient focus on design, organisations become self-serving. Effort goes into maintaining the status quo and optimising the existing model long after it ceases to serve either the organisation or its stakeholders. This works whilst the model remains relevant. However, the organisation becomes vulnerable and inevitably falls prey to competition with newer models.

There are alternatives to the traditional model. They constantly appear and disrupt marketplaces. For example, the model of online retail is quite different to the model of high street retail and as a result they have different sorts of problems. Online retail grew from a model used by mail order companies that struggled to gain market dominance. Information Technology became the enabler that addressed their problems. Now these IT solutions give considerable advantage to online retail. Its market presence escalated at the expense of traditional high street retailers who stuck with their existing model.

Creating a decentralised scalable model

Years of scaling their traditional model resulted in Matt Black Systems increasing costs and reducing flexibility, driving the organisation towards failure. The programs Andrew and Julian had tried were attempts to optimise each function but did not deliver the business-wide improvements they hoped for.

"As the business grew, more people were added to the functions, increasing the focus on functions and exacerbating the problems of silos. The rationale of the failed programs was to optimise our existing silo model. We assumed that by improving each function, overall efficiency would improve as a result. Seeing the organisation as a collection of functions and not as a whole was the 'Achilles heel' of these projects."

Instead of further attempts to improve their traditional model, they chose to pursue a new decentralised model. This aimed to integrate as many functions as possible into each cell and force them to be dealt with as one. The new approach could also reduce costs as there were fewer admin and management roles. Their hypothesis was that a decentralised model would remove the distraction of artificial boundaries between functions and allow people to focus on balancing their needs with those of customers and suppliers.

For the decentralised model to operate effectively, each cell had to be fully autonomous. This posed a significant problem. How would the communications and transactions between multifunctional cells be controlled?

The internal market

The migration of procurement into the multifunctional cells was the second step towards decentralisation. But it threw up many problems as well as successes. The cells had no formal way to exchange stock between them. Excess stock or bulk purchases were trapped in a cell. Also, with their increased sense of autonomy came an increased discontent with the performance of the remaining, centralised internal suppliers. As a result, Julian and Andrew developed a proper 'internal market' for the commercial exchange of goods and services between the multifunctional cells and the other internal operations. This formal system was essential because transactions taking place internally needed to be isolated from those with external customers and suppliers, as the tax and cash flow treatment were different.

"We introduced a simple and automated transaction system. Then we extended the internal market to all products and services exchanged internally, including admin ones. The multifunctional cells insisted that every internal product or service had to be quoted, contracted and paid for.

In response, the Accounts function charged £20 for processing every sales and purchasing invoice. This covered their costs. Soon cells questioned why

invoice processing was so expensive. The Accounts team said that £20
represented their costs and there was no choice.

The cells demanded responsibility for raising their own invoices and chasing
payments. This required an IT solution that was simple and efficient. Launch-
ing that system proved to be the start of the end for the Accounts Department."

Month upon month, the basic invoice processing work of the Accounts function reduced as the cells took on more of this role. To retain their revenue
and cover their costs, the Accounts function increased their prices and
offered more sophisticated accountancy services. This was counterproductive
as it accelerated the rate at which the cells took on the accountancy role.

Meantime, it was in the best interest of the cells to pay more attention to
their wider financial responsibilities. This reduced their expenditure and
increased their efficiency and profits. No one forced cells to take on these additional responsibilities, they demanded them to benefit from the reduction
in cost and the increase in their value-added bonus.

In the end, the cells took control of all their bookkeeping needs and only paid
for more sophisticated accountancy services, which they sourced externally. Andrew and Julian were surprised that this also reduced the outstanding debtors
and resulted in better management of creditors. The cells were more effective at
these routine financial tasks than the accounting specialists had been. The benefit to the cells was that the flow of goods was no longer disrupted by suppliers
withholding delivery because their previous bills had not been paid.

This pattern repeated itself for many of the internal services. In time, the
costs of the organisation fell dramatically. Primarily, because much of the
data that central functions had worked with was generated by the cells. First
the cell collected and collated the data and then passed it to the central
function, who in turn processed the data. The old approach involved a high
degree of 'double handling', the data being acted up on by both the cells and
the central function. The new approach removed this double handling.

From cost to price

Some unquestioned and unhelpful habits persisted. Ways of doing things that
had been established in simpler times were revered as sacrosanct "because we've
always done it this way". An example of this was 'cost-plus' pricing of goods to
customers. This was especially pertinent to the internal market because it would

be a mistake to base prices on costs which might be low or high. As a result, they might be cheaper or more expensive than outside suppliers. It was much more important that prices were set so they were competitive.

This shift in emphasis meant there was an improved understanding of the market price for products and services. Armed with this understanding, the question of the price offered to the customer was then simply whether they wanted to be above or below the market price.

The costs were under their control. Emphasis was placed on areas where cost improvements would have the greatest impact. The challenge was to make the product profitably, at the market price. Customers don't care about your costs.

This obvious and basic rule of sales and marketing came as a complete revelation to the team at Matt Black, who had come to expect their costs to be met whether they were high or low.

> *"Curiously, the admin and finance team had the most problem with this market price concept. They would consistently increase their prices to their internal customers without reference to the price of subcontracting these services outside the company. As a result, the cells increasingly used subcontractors or took on the responsibilities themselves. We would have imagined those who were most financially literate would have been better able to grasp this concept. In reality, they were the most resistant to the need to be competitive."*

A small program was set up to gather information from the market and to identify customer price expectations and competitor offerings. The results were shocking. In some instances, Matt Black were massively under-priced, whilst in others the opposite was true.

It took some time for behaviours to shift. Slowly people reduced the effort spent on calculating costs and increased the effort spent on reducing costs. In time, this cost reduction had a profound impact on performance. The organisation shifted to the question; "how could they turn a profit out of the price that was available without compromising quality?"

Complicated, and almost impossible, cost allocations and calculations were replaced with a simpler approach. The raw material costs were subtracted from the price to give an estimate of the value-added by the labour. This was then divided by the price to provide a ratio. The target was a minimum of 50%. The question then remained; how to get the job done within the available sum and leave a healthy profit.

Innovation was often required to make the best of these contracts. The perspective at Matt Black had reversed. Initially, prices varied and costs were considered fixed. Latterly the price was seen to be fixed by the external market and the internal costs had to respond accordingly.

Introducing a rudimentary P&L Account

Reviewing the situation, Andrew and Julian asked themselves if the financial performance of each multifunctional cell could be obtained from their sales and purchasing data by creating a primitive P&L Account.

To achieve this required the capture of every sale and purchase made by each cell and accounting for them properly. A rudimentary system had already been established, but this next step would be more rigorous and formal to better represent the financial transactions. This would not be easy but held the promise of transforming the financial literacy of everyone in the business.

New software was introduced to automate this process. This cut costs because the multifunctional cells had been reporting their transactions on spreadsheets. The added benefit was that the organisation had better financial data than ever before and it was available in real time.

With the introduction of this rudimentary P&L Account, Matt Black Systems could track the financial performance of each cell. Most importantly, this provided a way for individual members to be directly rewarded for their performance.

Reducing overheads

Many organisations attempt to calculate the true cost of internal services but few have gone as far as Matt Black Systems in creating an internal market. For example, the UK's National Health Service introduced a form of internal market, where different parts of the service cross-charge and private suppliers bid for work previously delivered by the NHS itself.

Subcontracting services is not new, but giving individual cells the autonomy to buy in 'overhead' functions such as accounts, quality, HR and general admin from external suppliers is a radical move. It is bound to meet resistance from people whose jobs are threatened or whose managerial importance will be diminished.

The status of managers in a hierarchy is dependent upon the size of their budget and the number of subordinates. There is little incentive for them to reduce costs as it is through the growth of their empire that they grow status. Thus, overheads grow rapidly in a silo structure. Introducing a genuine free market, reveals the true costs of all products and services, internal and external, including administrative ones. It facilitates comparison of internal providers with external ones and holds all to account.

Summary

- Most businesses scale through functionalisation.

- Most leaders do not see organisational design as part of their role.

- Andrew and Julian realised that the future of Matt Black Systems was to address the issues and adopt a more decentralised, autonomous and scalable model.

- An internal market was designed to facilitate transactions between the multifunctional cells.

- The internal market showed the true cost of central services and led to cells taking control of their own bookkeeping and ultimately to the demise of the Accounts Department.

- Moving from cost-plus pricing to market pricing was an essential part of introducing the internal market.

- Introducing a rudimentary P&L Account into the cells increased understanding of finances, which directly influenced behaviours.

FURTHER DECENTRALISATION

Chapter 6

The old and the new side by side

Organisations differ. Twenty-first century organisations are increasingly different to their twentieth century counterparts. They have different supply chains, new routes to market and different cost structures. For businesses to survive and thrive in the twenty-first century, they must take advantage of new opportunities or fall prey to more progressive competitors. Existing businesses have the advantage of an established foothold in a market but the disadvantage of an embedded, probably traditional, organisational model. They have the tricky task of transitioning from an old to a new model to stay relevant. They must change to new behaviours or failure will be inevitable.

The old order will have a culture of conformance, confining behaviours to those most familiar. During times of change, the culture rejects alternatives just as an immune system rejects foreign bodies. The bigger the shift demanded by the new order, the more foreign it appears and the greater the reaction of the 'organisational immune system'. Disruption caused by this rejection can threaten the survival of the organisation. Some people resist change to the bitter end and this was evident at Matt Black Systems.

> *"We found ourselves first protecting our experiments from rejection by the organisation. Then, with a new blueprint for the future, we protected the roll-out from rejection, until the entire company transitioned to the new model.*
>
> *This program split the organisation into two; the established group and the new multifunctional cells. The cell teams took on a broader role, embracing the idea of managing their own supply chains, ensuring the satisfaction of customer and supplier contracts. The legacy organisation continued to pursue their bounded roles and worked in much the same way as they always had."*

The multifunctional cells exercised their new control over their external supply chain. Their experience with the internal supply chain was far less successful. Time and again it was the internal, specialised, 'single source' supply that undermined their schedules. The cells invested in new equipment and skills to carry out as many of the specialised processes as possible and reduce their dependence on the internal suppliers.

Whilst this significantly reduced the workload of the internal suppliers, all too often their deliveries remained late. As a result, the centralised management and admin team didn't see a reduction in the burden of coordination. Meanwhile, the cells were delivering quickly and more reliably.

The gradual process of integration ran for a while in the hope that the remaining centralised functions would accept the multiskilled approach. The new approach was more productive, members better rewarded via their bonuses, and they were more satisfied with their work. It was evident to everyone that this was the new direction of the company.

Eventually progress halted. Most of what could be integrated into the multifunctional cells had been. What remained were activities dependent on specialised capital equipment and specialised skills, and they tenaciously resisted integration into the multifunctional cells.

The remaining bottlenecks were addressed

In time, just three of the internal specialists persisted. Andrew and Julian decided to improve the performance of the company further. Each of these specialists would become autonomous cells and adopt the management and admin responsibilities just like the other cells. They would be responsible for their customer and supplier contracts, and measured accordingly.

The existing multifunctional cells would no longer pass their remaining requirements to the production manager for him to arrange fulfilment. Instead they passed them directly to the internal specialist cells. This was not welcomed by the specialists who did not want to be measured financially nor to deal contractually with the multifunctional cells. They preferred their personable relationship with the production manager.

A tight rein on operations

From the beginning of the devolution process, the failures and blockages in other parts of the organisation became increasingly apparent. One early example was the behaviour of the production manager. He liked to keep a tight rein on operations. He disliked the cells managing their workload independently. He dealt with irate customers and couldn't use the resources of these cells as they were busy with their own commitments.

The production manager tried to maintain control by keeping the drawing and instruction sets, necessary to make the products, under lock and key. Access to these documents determined what work the cells could do. When he wanted a cell to focus on his priorities, he restricted access to the critical documents for their other work. This caused a problem for the cells and tensions grew.

The more customer contracts the cells took on, the greater the antics of the production manager. As the custodian of all the information he was critical to the start of every job. The issue became especially problematic when he went on vacation.

Despite their direct efforts, the cell teams could not get him to release control of the documents they needed. He was holding the organisation to ransom to ensure that he could use the cells to support his irate customers. He was just using whatever means he had to achieve the best outcome for his upset customers.

> *"When the production manager went on holiday, we unlocked the drawing cabinets and distributed the relevant documents to the appropriate cells where they would now be stored, much as we had previously done with the centralised stores. After this, the cells were able to operate much more autonomously.*
>
> *When the production manager returned and discovered his 'lost documents' we knew we would be forced into the decision whether to trust the internal market to coordinate itself without day-to-day centralised control or to reassert the control of the production manager. We chose the internal market.*
>
> *We suggested that the production manager take a role within one of the specialist cells, on his existing pay and conditions. He originally came up through the ranks of this specialisation and had the relevant skills. He also had the administrative ability that the cell was struggling with.*
>
> *But he already had plans to explore new opportunities and chose to leave the business. He started a new career in an entirely different sector."*

This started a rapid process of the cells resolving production tensions and constraints. The production manager had been using the good performing cells to assist with the poor performing internal specialised functions and their late deliveries.

This was an example of misdirection within the organisation. Problems in one place (internal, specialist cells) were projected elsewhere. The underlying problems were divided and spread around the organisation. The symptoms were easy to see, but determining the cause was difficult when they appeared so far from their source.

The opportunity for problems to be projected far away from their source was removed when the internal supply chain started to self-coordinate. Initially this produced seemingly new problems, but Andrew and Julian quickly identified many of these as not new at all. They were the root cause of many of the symptoms they had been battling for years.

Dividing the fixed costs

With the eventual extension of the multifunctional cell approach to all areas of the organisation, all fixed costs had to be factored into their basic P&L accounts. There were no remaining centralised functions that could be allocated these fixed costs.

> "We needed to define all the fixed costs and fairly distribute them across the cells. These included floor space, local taxes, insurance, electricity and upkeep. Initially there was considerable disquiet about this charge, especially from cells that consumed disproportionate amounts. Open negotiation meant the cells were able to agree upon their appropriate share."

Everyone assumed that the central admin team had negotiated good contracts with suppliers. However, once the charges passed to the cells, they found alternative suppliers and negotiated contracts offering significant savings. As more of the fixed charges were passed down to the cells, they proved themselves to be proficient at finding better deals and received the benefit for doing so.

Better but not good enough

Things were good, the backlog was almost gone and customers were significantly more content. There was a great improvement in performance; so much so that the company won awards. However, this reduced the ability for people on the trailing edge to earn the 'backlog bonus'. Without this incentive, their productivity started to plateau.

The change program had produced great results, averting a crisis. It was self-financing, sustainable, productive and capable of overcoming its own difficulties. It had powerful measurements of performance and was more profitable, even though the pay rates had significantly increased. Both culture and engagement had improved.

Andrew and Julian could have chosen to stop there, but their ambitions had grown and they wanted to perfect what they had started. Good enough was no longer good enough.

> *"The leading edge was working really well. What was left on the trailing edge was a couple of poor performing cells and the remaining back-office team who were managing the fixed costs. This team was now separated with a cell identity in our internal market. They were not responsible for any customer contracts unlike all the others who had external contracts. All that remained was for the poor performing cells and the admin cell to be reformed."*

A new success bonus

All cells could now adopt the value-added bonus scheme with its contract metrics. With the integration of the fixed costs into the cell finances, the value-add statement came to resemble a proper P&L account. This provided the opportunity to make another leap to a new bonus scheme. The cells agreed to fully integrate both their fixed costs and their labour costs to reflect their true profitability. This new bonus, based on individual multifunctional cell profitability, was more generous than the previous schemes.

> *"The new scheme didn't leave much 'headroom' to cover the loss-making cells, but it reflected the seriousness of our efforts to overcome the organisation's problems. It was a big carrot.*
>
> *The new bonus was a generous offer; but the barrier in negotiations was from the unprofitable cells. They would lose out. They would lose the bonus from working off any ongoing backlog and they would also lose because of their poor profitability.*
>
> *Eventually, a deal was struck where the bonus of the profitable cells would be capped at a level that was acceptable. The remaining balance would go into subsidising the loss-making cells."*

Summary

- Matt Black Systems evolved into two camps, the legacy team and the new multifunctional cells.

- As the new multifunctional cells became more autonomous and productive, it became evident that this was the direction the company would take.

- The production manager was proving to be a blockage. When he left, the cells no longer had to cover for poor performing internal specialist cells, exposing their poor performance.

- The fixed costs were passed to the cells via the internal market. When the charges hit the cells, they sought out better deals and made significant savings.

- A new success bonus scheme was introduced to replace the backlog bonus and the value-add bonus. The new bonus was based on the profitability of the individual multifunctional cell.

MAKING IT RIGHT

Chapter 7

Maintaining quality control

For many businesses, maintaining strict conformity and process control is essential to success. The prospect of decentralising and losing tight oversight of their operations is unimaginable. At the start of their turnaround Julian and Andrew shared this view.

The aerospace industry maintains safety standards with strict regulation. Customers are often involved in overseeing their supply chains and any problem attracts attention and increases scrutiny. For Matt Black Systems one particular incident towards the end of their failed Lean program proved a turning point in this story. That was the moment they redirected their focus onto improving compliance.

A product failure triggered a series of customer audits. The aim was to pinpoint where the process instructions failed and how the non-conforming product was passed along the supply chain.

> *"I was confident in our process instructions so when our customer demanded a copy, we duly sent it for assessment. Subsequently, the customer phoned to discuss the failure. They assessed our process instructions as premium quality and not the source of the fault. The instructions were far better than the product built using them. The customer concluded that our management and supervision must be at fault. The only explanation was a failure in conformance and compliance."*

This was a key experience as it directed their efforts away from further Lean projects. Perfect work instructions were wasted if compliance to them was the problem. They were forced to confront what was clearly a people problem; a cultural malaise.

The pursuit of this problem took Andrew and Julian away from the traditional Lean approach and towards generating more compliance. They already had high levels of supervision, so the difficulties indicated an 'engagement' problem rather than a lack of strict supervision. At that time, they had more supervision and management than ever. Increasing it would be unaffordable and wouldn't solve the underlying engagement problem.

An innovation in the Lean projects

The previous Lean projects had forced Matt Black Systems to capture and document their process instructions using job details. This was a challenge as small batch manufacture means the effort invested in detailed instructions could not be recouped by repeat work. Due to a work backlog in the team writing these instructions, sometimes the entire production run was complete before the instructions were generated. More often, the instructions were created whilst the parts were being built rather than before. The instructions were a build record rather than an instruction set, sometimes neither.

This was not their only concern about process instructions. Detailed process instructions tended to inhibit change. If a new piece of equipment or method was contemplated, its benefit was weighed against the cost of re-writing all the affected process instructions. The prohibitive time and cost of re-writing instructions discouraged small improvements. It was with these challenges in mind that Andrew and Julian created an innovative approach to resolve this problem.

They started with an experiment to prove the performance of the existing approach. They mapped in detail the processes for making a mug of tea. 27 separate steps were documented and each one allocated a time to complete. It was determined that a mug of tea would take five and a half minutes to make.

A mug of tea was then made exactly following the documented process. It took considerably less time than predicted. The kettle was still hot from a previous mug of tea which was not accounted for in the instruction details (see Bayes' Theorem below). More importantly however, the tea produced was not good. The process didn't control the quality of the tea. Further refinement followed and soon the instructions were so complicated that they were unusable. And this was just to produce a mug of tea!

Bayes Theorem (Rev. Thomas Bayes)

Refers to the probability of an event occurring based on knowledge of the prior conditions. This theory is the nemesis of planning and fixed instructions. It predicts that the probability of a plan succeeding improves as the plan progresses as long as there is no evidence to undermine it. Planning must be accompanied by surveillance and feedback. In practical terms, planning is a process not an event. Bayes theorem reminds us that planning only works when combined with the rigorous observation of changing circumstances.

The experiment proved that detailed process documentation was a flawed approach. An alternative was needed that could satisfy two conflicting requirements: Andrew's previous approach was to unambiguously document every process in pursuit of compliance whereas Julian's preferred approach was to leave the job to the operator and then check that the final outcome conformed to requirements.

Andrew doubted Julian's approach as it allowed process variation. Julian's problem with Andrew's approach was that exhaustive instructions didn't solve the compliance problem and would prove to be uneconomical.

Eventually, they devised a hybrid between process control and outcome control. They termed it their 'Gateway Review' method: each process was divided into chunks that produced an outcome. Each outcome was small enough that one person could do the work and re-work was the least wasteful. Between each outcome sat a gateway review (inspection or test activity). No part would pass through the gateway onto the following process without its conformance to requirements being confirmed.

This approach represented a significant increase in 'in-process' inspection and test, but a significant reduction in the detail of the process instructions. Julian felt this approach would free the operators to make process improvements and Andrew felt that the extra inspection would ensure quality. Special processes that needed to be controlled due to risk, could be included before the applicable gateway.

Once again, they conducted an experiment. They selected a product with previous problems and broke its instructions into discrete steps, with gateway reviews between the steps. They removed detailed process instructions and placed emphasis on defining, inspecting and testing quality at each process stage. Overall, the process details shrank in size whilst the gateway reviews increased.

Experimentation with the new approach revealed a large array of problems. Initially people carried on with their old habits, and the gateway reviews revealed multiple quality failures. For many, the new inspection regime was viewed as the cause of the new failures, yet it was simply discovering previously hidden problems. There were concerns that problems would be revealed that the operators couldn't resolve and they would be held accountable.

"In time, the burden of reworking faulty products encouraged changes in working practices. Eventually operations settled down to produce quality products, right first time. The consequences of process failure were now immediate and obvious to the operators and, in spite of their protests, they changed their habits.

It worked, and worked better than expected. Quality improved, rework reduced, old habits were broken and there was an inspection and test paper-trail that met the aerospace industry norms. Importantly, the operational costs were significantly lower. Whilst some of the previous costs of supervision were redirected towards increased inspection and test, overall, there was less support labour required.

Notwithstanding initial resistance, we were clear this new approach was achieving the outcome conformance and process compliance customers demanded. The approach would be rolled out throughout the cells. As re-work reduced, resistance fell away."

Introducing an overarching philosophy

After successfully introducing the gateway review method and enjoying its benefits, Andrew and Julian looked to apply it beyond operations. They wanted to bring the advantages of improved quality control to the administrative activities of the business.

"Our biggest challenge was that the gateway reviews in the admin processes were difficult to define without a customer to provide explicit requirements and quality expectations. The admin activities were mostly driven by external demands that could be considered as a sort of external 'customer'. We set about the task of explicitly defining the quality characteristics for these requirements and then linking all our admin processes to the laws and regulations that demanded them."

For example, time sheets were used for many administrative purposes, such as payroll and compliance with the working hours directive. The focus on the underlying regulations had been lost and admin processes had become self-serving, complicated and misdirected. On reflection, the administrative processes were in far worse order than the manufacturing instructions had been. The reorganisation and rationalisation of the administrative processes was a pivotal exercise. There were significant savings to be found and improvements in quality to be achieved. This project would have the added benefit of easing the devolution of admin into the cells.

The application of the gateway review approach throughout the organisation resulted in the need to rationalise and standardise the technique. This provided many advantages: more consistency, reduced costs, complete and thorough application and rapid familiarisation.

Requirements: Say-Do-Prove

In making the gateway review scheme more generic, to work with many different applications, its scope had to be extended to the external demands on the organisation, such as customer contracts, laws or regulations. This increase in scope, beyond the limitations of manufacturing demands, forced every process to be viewed in its widest context rather than in isolation.

For the administration activities, the requirements were mandatory (statutory, regulatory and contractual). Whilst for production, requirements were discretionary commitments agreed with customers and suppliers. Exactly how these would be met by the business, was a matter of design and planning.

For operations, a 'declaration of intent' was made. In simple terms this was a product design, process instructions, gateway reviews, final test, records to be kept, and a production schedule. Each part had its direct equivalent in the administrative realm. Together, this declaration of intent became known as their 'Say'. Each was 'saying' how their requirements were to be met.

The day-to-day activities, adhering to the schedule, following the instructions, passing through the gateway reviews, final test and generating the associated records were all part of doing a good job. This became known as the 'Do'. Each was 'doing' what they had committed to in the Say, whether that be processing a product or carrying out a Health & Safety Assessment.

Finally, the paper trail of records generated provided evidence of the successful satisfaction of a contract or of compliance to a law or regulation. The retrieval of these records and their integration into reports and statutory submissions came to be collectively known as 'Prove'. Evidence presented proved that commitments had been honoured.

'Requirements: Say-Do-Prove', the shorthand for this approach, could be applied to every part of the organisation.

Implementation of this singular approach

The production gateway reviews were re-ordered to align with this new format. Each set of instructions and inspection criteria were assembled using an identical approach. Folders were created with the requirements explicitly defined at the beginning, followed by instructions and drawings then the gateway reviews, final inspection criteria and templates for all the records that would be required. The folder was completed with a contents page and integrated into a single document control system that kept track of the versions of every document in the folder as well as every folder in the entire system.

As the program took shape and people became comfortable and familiar with the Requirements: Say-Do-Prove folders, they became informally known simply as Recipes. This term was formally adopted to encourage familiarity. The singular approach that was used to standardise the creation and format of all Recipes was formalised into a Meta-recipe, becoming known as the 'Recipe for creating Recipes'.

> *"For the cells, this approach was not really new, it was an extension of what they were already doing in their production operations. However, because we were also applying it to administrative processes, the approach was initially greeted as entirely new.*
>
> *We conducted an experiment as the cells integrated the administration. We were keen to see if our Recipe approach was applicable to every part of the administrative operations. Our first step was to apply it to single tasks in quality, accounts and governance.*
>
> *In each case it worked. However, the number of problems uncovered was more than when the system was applied to operations. For us this was positive, as it revealed the admin functions to be ripe for cost-saving and efficiency improvements. The organisation would benefit greatly from resolving the dysfunctions that had built up over many years in the admin system."*

Many of the problems revealed by their experiment were intertwined with other admin tasks away from the experimental ones. It became clear that their administrative system was far more interdependent than the production operations were. To resolve the admin system required all its parts to be tackled as a whole, rather than working through each process in turn.

Reforming their administration system was the largest project they had tackled; so large it could easily overwhelm them.

Summary

- For many organisations, strict conformity and process control is seen as a block to operator autonomy.

- The gateway review approach improved quality control and highlighted issues that required remedy.

- The removal of detailed process instructions and the feedback from gateway reviews led to vigorous process improvement.

- The wider philosophy of 'Requirements: Say-Do-Prove' allowed the gateway review approach to be extended to administrative processes.

- A Meta-recipe was produced, a Recipe for creating Recipes that set a standard for all Recipes. Critically this demanded the declaration of requirements and ensured processes served their wider context.

DEVOLVING BUREAUCRACY

Chapter 8

The final leap into decentralisation

The administration function was the biggest remnant of centralisation in the business. Its holistic reform was a large and disruptive project requiring Andrew and Julian to give it careful consideration.

The aim was to make each cell an autonomous business, a microcosm of the business as a whole. With separate administration in each cell, reform would progress one cell at a time. The reform of the first cell would act as an exemplar for the reform of the rest. With this complete, each cell could provide a suite of admin data to be aggregated and reported for the business as a whole. This bottom-up approach turned a large and potentilly disruptive project into one that was manageable and low risk.

With this plan in hand, the initial task was to create a 'recipe book' covering every administrative requirement, translated into individual Recipes for the operation of the first autonomous cell. Once the Recipes were being followed and proven, the approach could be rolled out with confidence.

The admin Recipes, just like the operational Recipes, included gateway reviews. This meant that there was a paper trail that demonstrated compliance with laws and regulations. It also satisfied the fiduciary duties of the directors. This admin project finally removed all barriers to full decentralisation.

Designing a cell admin system

Andrew and Julian found that there is surprisingly little guidance available for organisations who wish to re-design their admin. New businesses often make up processes as they stumble across each requirement. This lack of guidance was unexpected as, although businesses are unique, their admin demands are similar. Company law, contract law, employment law, tax law etc apply equally to every organisation within a jurisdiction. A simple off the shelf system might be expected, but only separate solutions to individual requirements such as Accounts, HR and the like are available.

> *"We brought together the fundamental laws that bounded our administration, into an exhaustive set of 'requirements' for a unified admin system. We also included the quality management requirements for our industrial sector. Once collected, we saw common patterns.*

With the requirements brought together in this way, it was clear that many were duplicated but used different vocabulary. As an example, we found inspection was labelled differently depending on the functional view point:

- *in accounts inspection was an 'audit'*
- *in human resources inspection was an 'appraisal'*
- *in sales inspection was a 'contract review'*
- *in design inspection was a 'design review'*
- *in development inspection was a 'first article inspection'*
- *in purchasing inspection was an 'acceptance check'*
- *in production inspection was a 'final test'*

The historic translation of the requirements within each function had led to specialist language being introduced for almost identical activities."

The holistic redesign taking place at Matt Black made it clear that requirements could be synthesised and condensed into common components. The advantage was that a single solution could be designed and applied to satisfy the many different functions. After gathering and synthesising all the requirements, they now had a set of demands for the design brief for their new holistic admin framework. It also became obvious at this point, that their legacy model did not satisfy this brief, so no wonder the organisation was in trouble.

It was not entirely clear what an alternative model might look like. The requirements within the design brief precluded many traditional approaches. The old solutions relied upon extensive managerial, supervisory and administrative overheads that were cost prohibitive.

"We felt we had few options whenever we asked ourselves 'how would a one-person business approach this problem?' Eventually, it became clear that the answer to our constraints lay in this very question. Distilling the complexity of the entire model to the level of a single individual provided a valid solution to the design brief. It condensed all the requirements to their simplest form. This removed the burden of cross-level (hierarchy) and cross-functional communication implicit in the traditional organisational model with its high levels of specialisation, management and supervision."

An attractive aspect of constraining the admin and management around an individual is that costs would vary depending upon the work undertaken. Simple work required little admin, whilst complex projects required more.

So, admin and management costs remained tightly associated with the needs of the job. By contrast, the traditional approach divides admin and management into many specialities, capable of addressing the most complex jobs. For less complex work, this cost burden outweighs the benefits of the division of labour. It is difficult to make the cost burden of traditional admin and management flex with the needs of each particular job. One size must fit all.

A methodical approach

To cover all aspects of the organisation's admin and management would involve hundreds of Recipes. To help cell teams locate a particular Recipe they needed, a system map was developed. Each Recipe was categorised as either Operational or Administrative. The Operations were broken down into Sales, Design and Production, whilst Admin was divided into HR, Accounts, Planning, Quality, Safeguarding and Governance.

This system map provided a place for the individual Recipes and became invaluable in providing a holistic overview of the entire model. This proved essential in bounding the project and ensuring it functioned as a whole. Work could be carried out on each 'small picture' Recipe without compromising its 'big picture' context.

> *"At the end of the project we had a library of hundreds of individual Recipes that covered all the tasks undertaken by the cell and together they formed a coherent whole. Dealing simultaneously with the detail and the overview was essential to making a success of this project. The devil does not just lie in detail.*

> *For the productive Recipes, the gateway reviews were a simple extension of the familiar testing and inspection regime. By contrast, adding gateway reviews to admin and management activities was an entirely new concept.*

> *There was resistance. Initially, resistance by the pilot cell who saw the extra admin as a burden and by the remnants of the centralised admin teams as they lost influence over the cell. During the pilot phase, it became obvious that the gateway reviews of the admin Recipes were not carried out as rigorously as for the operational Recipes.*

> *It was at this time we decided to devolve the audit function to an independent contractor. A monthly audit was introduced, carried out by a third party, to oversee all the gateway review records. This was irrespective of whether they*

were operational or administrative records. This was critical to maintaining con-
formance. Our internal auditor had been far too susceptible to social influence"

From this point on, conformance of the pilot cell consistently exceeded the
level previously achieved by the centralised functions. Critically, costs were
also significantly lower. In addition, as with the productive Recipes, the admin Recipes entered a cycle of continuous improvement. Improvements were
driven by the problems identified at the gateway reviews. Costs continuously
reduced and compliance continuously improved.

Roll out

The pilot cell was critical in road-testing the reforms. They problem-solved
and de-bugged the Recipes. As a result, they were invaluable in reducing
the program risks and avoiding unforeseen pitfalls. The pilot scheme was a
success. The pilot cell was significantly more compliant, had higher product
quality and lower costs.

The program was ready to roll out to the other cells, with the exception of
what remained of the central admin cell, which became a stranded asset. As
each new cell transformed, the flow of information to the centralised admin
cell diminished. As each of the centralised systems became redundant, they
were decommissioned. Eventually nothing was left. All the admin and management was devolved to the cells.

As the demand for central admin dried up, there was no work for the admin
team and they either left the company or found new roles in the cells. This
last phase again saw a significant drop in costs and an increase in productivity
(sales per person).

The impact on the cells

Some cells responded to their new autonomy more effectively than others.
Some eagerly addressed their problems and dug into their root causes. Things
improved dramatically for them. Others struggled with the freedom and
their performance languished. Those that didn't respond rigorously, were
stuck in an unending stream of small problems. The audit regime highlighted and pinpointed this poor performance, making it clear which cells were
not performing and the specific nature of their failings. This was equally
evident in both their operational and their administrative activities.

"The cells containing more legacy staff tended to perform worst. Over the previous decades the organisation had encouraged a shift from exercising skills, to following instructions. Perhaps this was to improve compliance, perhaps in response to micro-management by the supervisory staff. Whatever the reason, a legacy of habits severely restricted the ability of some staff to embrace the current changes.

These legacy behaviours were additionally encouraged by the structures and systems previously in place. On reflection we realised many of our problems had been self-imposed. Previously the management team had reacted to issue after issue in isolation, imposing changes which had introduced perverse incentives and unintended consequences. Thoughtless processes were instituted, in response to a crisis, without sufficient consideration of the conflicts and contradictions generated. Not only did this hinder the system as a whole, it also had a cultural impact."

As centralised systems were reinvented and devolved into the multifunctional cells, the project revealed its full decentralised nature.

Summary

- Centralised administrative tasks were the primary block to autonomy of cells.

- A system map was developed to provide an overview of the developing model. This approach facilitated the holistic redesign of all the admin as a manageable project.

- The review of each admin process provided a great opportunity for cost savings and productivity improvements.

- Recipes were applied to all admin tasks and a pilot cell became a microcosm of the business as a whole. The pilot cell de-bugged the admin and management Recipes and reduced the risk of the program.

- The new approach was rolled out and the cells embraced it, making significant improvements. The remaining central functions could then be disbanded.

- Cells with more legacy staff struggled the most to embrace the new approach.

RECIPES FOR SUCCESS

Chapter 9

Sorting out poor performance

The universal rollout of Recipes saw a flurry of process improvements and innovations. Progress was clear. All the preparatory work that went into the Recipe system and the improvements in the pilot project were at last paying dividends across the whole business.

Improvement in profitability was not limited to cost reductions. Cell capacity also increased as a result of productivity improvements. They were doing more with less. The situation was not perfect, but the success was clear. Cell teams wanted to reduce their work by maximising process efficiency whilst making sure they passed gateway reviews. Between the inspection 'book ends' people searched for waste to eliminate and found new ways to make their lives easier. The success bonus, based on cell profitability, was not the only motivator but it helped.

> *"Cell teams were making changes themselves. They focussed on new jigs, fixtures, tools and arrangements to improve production. The cells implemented Lean tools themselves to increase profit and thus success bonus and to make their jobs easier and more predictable.*
>
> *This adoption of Lean tools, rather than consultants imposing them, was more effective in reducing rework and increasing productivity. Things were done correctly, predictably and productively. There was now a logical benefit for the Lean tools within the cells. Sadly, this success was not reflected in every cell. Some cells still performed badly and audit increasingly revealed their shortfalls against the Recipe system. They were dogged by numerous minor problems. In the trail-blazing search for a workable solution, our focus had rightly been on the leading edge of change. Now it was time to turn our attention to the trailing edge of the organisation; those parts that were still performing poorly on many measures."*

These trailing cells had unhappy customers, poor financial performance and struggled with passing their work through the gateway reviews. Audit revealed that administrative operations were equally sporadic. These cells were characterised by a multitude of broken promises. Commitments were made, to suppliers, customers and colleagues, and were not met.

Though individually, each broken promise was a minor issue, together they created chaos. For the first time, Matt Black Systems, through their decentralised approach, could pinpoint the source of this swarm of minor issues. It was time to focus on those cells where failures were still occurring.

Addressing the shortfalls revealed by audit

The first attempt at addressing the poor performing cells was a reversion to the old ways of thinking. Many habits had persevered in the poor performing cells; they hadn't embraced the opportunities. Training and coaching was attempted to improve their ability to address their own problems in the same way as the successful teams were doing. Significant money was spent on training 'best practice' gleaned from outside the company and from the high performing cells within. At first, this investment seemed to make a difference. Apparently, a workable solution had been found and the number of small problems decreased. However, as soon as training ceased, small problems crept in again, and were revealed by audit. Profitability never improved in these lagging cells. Training and coaching hadn't worked before and again it wasn't working.

After failing with these traditional methods, Andrew and Julian rethought how to address a seemingly intractable problem. They had learned that making changes to the ruleset of the cells achieved positive results. But when rules worked well in other cells there was no point in changing them for failing cells. Something else was going on.

Something was prohibiting improvement in the poor performing cells, but it had now been isolated from the other cells. Perhaps an alternative approach could be introduced to further confine the problems? So, instead of trying to identify the causes, they chose to split the poor performing cells into separate smaller cells. Then they could see if each new cell continued to suffer equally or whether the problems would be further isolated. This division was also in line with their overall objective of further decentralisation (making the cells smaller and smaller).

> *"The next question was 'what do we do with the poorly performing cells?' By now, the answer was obvious; we split them again. This we continued to do, until we reached a cell of just two people. At this stage we had many more cells and only a few were performing poorly. We took this experiment to its logical conclusion and divided the poor performing cells again, leaving just one person in each.*
>
> *We were anxious about the practicality of this, yet this resolution was taking us in the direction we imagined: a network of autonomous, single person multifunctional cells. This final push into total decentralisation (down to the individual rather than cell teams) was introduced for pragmatic reasons and not in the pursuit of a grand plan."*

Having split the poor performing cells, most of them showed a material improvement. Poor performance continued in a few and audit revealed a continuous stream of problems. Not only were they failing audit, but they were also making heavy losses. By contrast, many of their former colleagues were on a path of continuous improvement and success. The poor performance seemed to be following particular people and not particular work.

Dividing up the work

Splitting the organisation into many smaller cells introduced a new dynamic; choice. Within larger cells there was agreement about the distribution of work. Some tasks 'belonged' to certain people. As the cells divided further, work was formally divided via customer contracts, not by the previous tacit agreements. Typically, each cell member chose a portfolio of contracts. This voluntary choice drove many cell members to adopt a more multiskilled role to complete their contracts. They had been resisting this within the old cell. Some people didn't want to work this way and chose to leave. Others enthusiastically settled into the opportunity. A few neither left nor grasped the opportunity. Their performance remained poor.

If the cell served internal customers, then their poor performance meant their colleagues looked elsewhere for a supplier, one who lived up to their promises. The rules of the internal market allowed each cell to choose where they sought internal services. Consequently, cells voted with their order books. Poor performers quickly ran out of work and became stranded.

> *"The audit failures and financial crisis brought the issue to a head. Poor performers told us that audit failures were 'not their fault', it wasn't their responsibility to resolve them, and that the financial loss wasn't their problem either. They were not paid to worry about this sort of stuff. If their work wasn't good enough then their training must have been at fault.*
>
> *They considered that their commitment only extended to making themselves available for work every day. They were not willing to make any promise with regard to their work, other than to be available to do what they were told. They pointed out that there was no requirement in their employment contract compelling them to offer any sort of promise or commitment to the quality, consistency or timeliness of their work."*

In common with most traditional businesses, the employment contracts at Matt Black were statements of the company rules for which the employees could be held to account. But as is so often the case, these rules were mainly prohibitions. The role descriptions within the contracts did not hold the individual accountable to customer or regulatory requirements.

> *"We realised that this needed to be resolved. However unpalatable, we were forced to micro-manage the situation. In a few cells we amended their Recipes to include detailed task instructions and supervisory oversight. This broke the rules of our gateway review approach but it was a pragmatic response to intransigence."*

The amended Recipes in these few cells were explicitly detailed. They left no doubt what was required of the operator. The operators were involved in creating detailed instructions and undergoing any training required. Frequently Julian and Andrew found that ambiguity or incompleteness in the details were used as an excuse for failure and non-performance. Each time, the Recipes were updated to eliminate the discrepancies until they were sufficiently extensive that only wilful avoidance could lead to failure.

Managing poor performance

The gateway reviews continued to reveal inconsistency in the work of certain operators, one day they would work rigorously the next day not. With highly detailed process instructions in place, once again the focus shifted from the accuracy of the instructions to variations in the performance of operators. Because the details of the operation were explicitly defined, errors were clear issues of role performance, for which the operator could be held accountable under their existing employment contract. This onerous approach could not have been applied to the business as a whole. It worked in a few cells because they were given work that was stable and long term. This meant the deployment of more prescriptive Recipes was appropriate but came at a cost. The other cells had customer contracts that regularly changed in size and complexity as is the nature of bespoke work. In these cases the investment in prescriptive Recipes would not have been worthwhile.

This process of micro-managing poor performing cells became known as 'Rescue and Recovery'. Its intention was to recover performance to the level of the other cells. Critically it held people accountable for the promises they made. Poor performing operators either improved or left the company.

Those that left released work that was eagerly drawn into other cells as it was the most stable and reliable work in the business.

As each poor performing cell was closed, the detailed Recipes were returned to their gateway review form, allowing their new owners to apply their talents more freely. The closure of poor performing cells meant overall productivity rose again, backlogs were reduced and overall profitability improved further. Unhappy customers became happy.

> "As a result, we reviewed all the employment contracts. A formal obligation to commit to the requirements of each role was added, as well as to be held accountable for the outcomes produced. This signalled that the time for experimentation was over.
>
> 18 months previously we began with an overtime experiment and extended it to embrace and disrupt many working practices. Step by step the changes were discussed and agreed, but until now, not formally captured. The new employment contracts formalised these changes. In addition, we included the new profit-based success bonus, along with a rationalised and simplified basic pay scheme. This meant a pay raise for all.
>
> In the new employment contract, we replaced the old disciplinary process, including the verbal and written warnings, with a new Rescue and Recovery process that also met the requirements of employment law. Any operator who failed was required to formulate a self-improvement plan, to identify educational needs and to submit to a much higher level of audit. When we needed to apply the policy, the operator's income would be subsidised and upon its successful conclusion they would once again be authorised to re-join the internal market as an independent cell."

In future, people would rarely spend long in this process. They would either quickly address the shortfalls that drew them into Rescue and Recovery, or claim the subsidised pay until they found another job. In hindsight, a few people within the old team had established a secure position within certain cells, even though they were not up to the demands of their role. They had been the source of many small problems that reverberated throughout the organisation and disrupted their colleagues.

As for the business results, operations became more compliant and consistent. The absence of re-work saw productivity rise, along with reduced firefighting and stress. Costs also reduced and work-life improved for everyone.

Dividing problem cells to the point where there was just one person in each, had isolated the problems. The better performing parts went on into a cycle of improvement as if relieved of a constraint.

Would this cell division approach provide similar benefits if it were applied to the good performing cells in the business?

Summary

- Small, seemingly insignificant, problems were aggregating into big ones.

- The Recipe approach provided a clear indication where the small problems were occurring.

- The leading edge were making promises and keeping them, whilst the trailing edge were making promises and breaking them.

- Where problems persisted, support and training were tried but were ineffective.

- Further division of poor performing cells identified the people opposed to making commitments for which they could be held to account.

- A formal program to micro-manage poor performing cells resulted in the removal of the remaining sources of broken promises and became the basis of Rescue & Recovery to replace the previous disciplinary system.

- Employment contracts were updated to reflect the 'do's' rather than the 'don'ts'. Increased profitability meant people could receive more pay for these extra demands.

LEAVING THE BUILDING

Chapter 10

Progressing well

Things at Matt Black Systems were positive. There were loose ends to tie up and each unfinished project had the potential to cause disruption. For example, the internal market was still in its formative stage. Basic administration was resolved, but like any unregulated market there were opportunities for exploitation and misdirection. As people became more familiar with its dynamics, they became more likely to start gaming it. Checks and balances were needed to close its loopholes. There was a mountain of work remaining for recovery to be sustained.

The Recipe approach had been very successful in streamlining activities. Operator engagement had clearly increased. The flow of day-to-day operations had improved significantly and the atmosphere felt calmer and more organised. Productivity was up and so was profitability.

> *"The days of pushing the organisation were over. Instead, change was being generated from within and our role switched to adjusting the model rather than creating it. Isolating and addressing poor performing individuals released others from their influence and operations improved enormously. Behaviours quickly adapted to the new model and contractual promises were now being made and kept. Lots of change was occurring, but there were still problems to address.*
>
> *Some changes were becoming dysfunctional as people explored their freedoms but without consideration of the wider impact. The organisation was feeling its way in a new environment but in the early days didn't possess a mature overview to guide individual decisions. This only came with experience. Nevertheless, we considered many of these mistakes could have been avoided if our model had basic checks and balances. The loopholes and perverse incentives within the model were our responsibility and not the fault of the staff that pushed the boundaries. In many ways the team were doing us a kindness, they were clearly signalling where improvements were needed."*

A few activities still needed to be decentralised, including the statutory requirements of the business. These would provide the big picture boundaries for the individual cells in accordance with the big picture/small picture approach favoured by Andrew and Julian. These boundaries would prevent the 'small picture' activities of the cells straying into dysfunction.

> "The initial goal of the model was to overcome poor compliance and conformance without micro-management. The Recipe system improved quality, increased the engagement of operators and processes continuously improved. People were demonstrating a high degree of self-management, yet they would still turn to us for approval. We didn't want to be the judge of each change taking place. Somehow, we had to both get out of the way, yet also ensure the changes were sensible. Our focus remained on the model, setting overarching boundaries to align everyone in a common direction but allow them to choose their own path."

Further division into cells of one

Division of the poor performing cells produced substantial benefits. As the cells became smaller, the few poor performing individuals were increasingly exposed and fell into Rescue and Recovery. Expanding on the success of cell division, the same approach was now applied to the remaining cells in the business.

> "In hindsight, hot-spots of non-compliance and poor performance had been the heart of our problem. The old organisational model meant these hot-spots were uncontained and able to spread their disruption throughout the organisation. In time it became clear that the hot-spots of disorder were associated with a few individuals. The old structure made it difficult to identify these people, although the teams subsequently revealed they had been aware of their weak members."

Dividing a good cell

As the cell division progressed, the contract metrics revealed these sub-cells had a wide range of performance; from acceptable to astonishing. It became clear that the ambitious high performers were engaged and eager for further change. Month after month, with their new freedoms they delivered consistently brilliant results, way beyond the expectations of Julian and Andrew. This program showed that cell division was equally beneficial to the best performing cells.

Attention focussed on cells needing most improvement to determine whether their performance was a reflection of their contracts or their operator approach. Time and again the personal factors of the individual in the cell proved to be fundamental.

*"These developments caused a new wave of personnel change. The people best
suited to the emerging model became further engaged and self-expressed. Those
least suited struggled and looked for opportunities elsewhere. The least suited
were invariably those whose overall performance was simply 'ok' despite putting
in more time and effort. Success seemed easy for some but elusive to others.*

*We could see that the pressures some felt were a direct result of the new mod-
el. We supported those it didn't suit with time and freedom to seek new opportunities outside the company. In one case this meant supporting someone
to start a business of their own, becoming an external supplier rather than
an internal supplier. Paradoxically, this was the very responsibility they had
been resisting whilst in the job."*

Integrating the big picture

In all organisations there are activities which are driven by 'big picture'
considerations. Negotiating prices, balancing productive capacity, making
compromises, taking risks and seizing opportunities are all things that go
beyond the normal boundaries of day to day concerns. Traditionally, the
responsibility for these wider concerns falls to managers or directors.

*"Without holding these higher concerns, the cells were not fully aligned with
the needs of the company. Therefore, they could not rise to the degree of
autonomy being demanded by the best performers. If these concerns were met
by the cells, there would be an opportunity to strike an even better financial
deal. Introducing checks and balances prevented cells from taking excessive
risks, over-charging their clients or otherwise exploiting them in pursuit of
those extra rewards.*

*The challenge for us was to formally define these overarching obligations
that the whole organisation had to meet. Obligations to creditors, fiduciary
obligations of directors, obligations in the Company's Act, those of HR law
and Generally Accepted Accountancy Principles. All these obligations were
explicitly defined and integrated into Recipes to properly devolve them into
the cells."*

Conceiving the cells as virtual companies

Once these final parts were added to the Recipe library, it was clear that
Recipes dealing with the productive operations at Matt Black Systems were

in a minority. Most Recipes were concerned with general admin, legal and regulatory requirements, or the overarching obligations. The Recipe library was therefore applicable to any company. It was a blueprint for devolving admin and obligations in any organisation.

> "We now had a Recipe library that properly bounded each cell within Matt Black Systems and an approach that could be applied to help any organisation. We had created a devolved model where the cells were mini versions of the company as a whole; even to the extent that each cell had a P&L Account and would soon have a Balance Sheet. We came to see our cells as virtual companies."

All through the turnaround program, Andrew and Julian had forced themselves to approach each stage from two different perspectives; the big picture and the small picture. They first summarised the situation and established its 'flavour' and direction. The second focussed on technical details and represented how the projects were actually 'put on the ground'. Spells of focussed attention were punctuated by wider evaluation, to identify the direction of their developments.

> "It was similar with metrics. Contract metrics had served us well, but they were inadequate to fully constrain the changes ahead. We could see that, as more was devolved to the cells, they were taking on the obligations of the whole business. Each appeared as a virtual company. This insight allowed us to add financial measures to the existing cell metrics. These measures would reflect the virtual company approach rather than simply the budget of a work cell."

Contract Measures

To be sustainable, the goal of the company was to 'enhance prosperity by forming contracts and satisfying them, successfully'. This statement embraced financial, ethical and professional dimensions. Seeing the cells as virtual companies meant integrating these 'big picture' factors within a new set of measures.

The new contract Measures were summarised as:
*   Individual Prosperity (e.g. salary & bonus)
*   Value of Formed Contracts (e.g. outstanding order value)
*   Value of Satisfied Contracts (e.g. sales over a period)
*   Success (e.g. surplus or profit of the cell)

These new measures were piloted in a single cell and the results monitored. They were an effective synthesis and gave people the freedom they demanded combined with tough business objectives. For the pilot cell this was a double edged sword, the rigour demanded was a curse, whilst the opportunity for reward and personal growth was seen as a blessing.

> *"The pilot was essential to explore the boundaries of the social contract under-pinning employment. Devolving more to the cell provided opportunities, yet they came with extra demands. It was unpredictable how individuals would react to adding these wider demands to their day to day contractual responsi-bilities. Would they regard these big picture demands as 'not their problem'?"*

For most people the opportunities for reward and personal growth out-weighed the added burdens. Those with the most insight saw that job losses would result if the company failed to satisfy these big picture demands. To maintain job security these burdens had always been 'their problem'. For them, the demands were not really new, they had simply become explicit rather than implicit.

The measures were rolled out to all the remaining cells and helped to distin-guish who was adding net value to the business. They showed, on balance, whose contribution was greater than their consumption. They also identified individuals adding disorder; those whose contribution was less than their consumption. The measures were more rounded than the previous metrics as they encompassed the formation of contracts and the emergent profitability. The value and volume of promises made, kept or broken were captured and displayed on a monthly basis.

Revealed by the measures

The measures impacted behaviours. For those who embraced these freedoms, new avenues for problem solving were opened. Smarter compromises were struck and average productivity soared. As an example, during sales negotiation clients were steered towards products that the cells were skilled in making.

Individual profits rose and the bonuses awarded for success grew accord-ingly. The new employment contract had explicitly devolved the big picture burdens to everyone. In return people were rewarded for shouldering them. Pay increased for everyone; for some it doubled. Money, however, was not the only reward. Taking individual ownership of these big picture burdens had a palpable impact on self-esteem and confidence.

"There seemed a visible shift in demeanour which was hard to describe. People seemed to be walking taller, using more forthright language and were more confident. We didn't understand how, but they seemed to extract extra personal meaning from their work that wasn't there before.

After what we observed could be best described as the transformation from self-management to self-leadership."

Self-management v Self-leadership

Self-management, a common goal for many progressive organisations, allows for only limited freedom for the employee. They are given a job to do and can decide how best to do it. If true autonomy is the goal then this can only be achieved through self-leadership. By contrast, in self-leadership, no one has a job imposed upon them. The choice of job, how it is to be done and how it integrates with others is entirely up to the individual. The employee thus has higher concerns in self-leadership which include for their personal goals and their financial imperative.

Introducing the Balance Sheet

To complete the transformation of the cells into virtual companies, a Balance Sheet was required. This would identify those company resources under the stewardship of each cell.

The existing company Balance Sheet was divided between all the virtual companies. The machines, equipment, cash, creditors and debtors stewarded by each was evaluated. Their Balance Sheet allowed them to control the cell's assets and liabilities.

"Using these Balance Sheets, we could confirm that the cells were not converting the company's assets into pay but were generating their income through productive endeavours. Finally, the Balance Sheets meant we could charge the cells for the capital they utilised. The charge also encouraged entrepreneurial behaviours, rather than allowing the cell to sit on accumulated profits as a buffer against hard times. The skills developed would be a far more valuable buffer in hard times than simply consuming retained earnings.

This introduction of the Balance Sheet again revealed a significant difference between cells. Some utilised significant capital while others were frugal. Some generated high returns whilst others barely covered the costs of their capital."

This later phase was laborious but the effort paid dividends. The organisation, with limited input from Andrew and Julian, became more financially literate and further improved the promises made by the cells. Instead of asking themselves whether they could take on a contract, they asked on what terms they should take it on.

An unexpected bonus from the introduction of the Balance Sheets was that within six months, more than 50% of the working capital was released from operations. This was a remarkable achievement, as Julian and Andrew had no idea of the extent to which operations were so over-invested.

Transformation to bottom-up

For the first time ever, every aspect of the overall performance of the company was derived by aggregating the performance of the individual cells or virtual companies as they were becoming known. No measures originated from the top-down.

> *"Gingerly at first, we encouraged decision-making autonomy within the virtual companies. This proved to be fruitful; quality improved and rework reduced as fewer mistakes were made.*
>
> *Whilst the chronic day to day mistakes had decreased, the problems associated with development and experimentation came to the forefront. These had little impact on operations. They were a healthy sign of exploration and continuous improvement.*
>
> *People became experimental and speculative and, as a result, our long-standing processes were improved. The Recipe system and measures had removed chronic mistakes from day-to-day operations whilst encouraging exploration and change."*

Inevitably there were failures, yet the Recipe system and measures ensured they were calculated risks. Failure became an inevitable part of exploration, rather than something to be avoided. Speculative projects were reviewed for 'the consequences of failure'. This entered into common language for projects as being 'crashworthy'. If the worst occurred, would the cell easily absorb the impact?

As individual growth accelerated, so did the organisation's ability to predict and resolve its challenges. It became proactive rather than reactive and was more robust, resilient and responsive.

"We grew confident in the capability of the organisation. More than that, our presence in the building was holding back the growth of the people within. They were unwilling to make decision independently whilst we remained on hand. We realised that it was time to leave and the moment was a critical step in the growing autonomy. We had to grasp it with courage. We chose to pack up our office, leave the building and no longer have a place within. We never returned. From this point the monthly measures and metrics were our only contact."

Once Andrew and Julian had left the building, the organisation was forced to become more self-reliant. At this moment it blinked into life as an independent organism reacting to its own internal feedback. In time it established an autonomy and personality all of its own. This triggered a process of self-induced change that took it in a direction and momentum all of its own. What emerged was an ecosystem with a personality quite independent from the individuals within, one with its own particular concerns and proclivities. This independence led to new progress, initially slow but as time passed confidence grew and progress accelerated. At times it even surprised its own members. For a decade this emergent ecosystem has been in charge of Matt Black and has shown itself to be proficient and professional. It has flourished in spite of the challenges it has encountered.

Summary

- Andrew and Julian further divided the remaining cells and this too resulted in better performance. They continued down this route to one-person cells.

- The 'big picture' obligations of the company were devolved into the individual cells. This involved a further set of Recipes, turning each cell into a fully autonomous 'virtual company' within the wider statutory company.

- Virtual companies provided their own 'top level' measures that were aggregated and reported.

- In pursuit of autonomy self-management was not enough, self-leadership became the goal.

- A Balance Sheet was introduced for each cell and charges made for the capital employed. This increased the financial literacy of the staff and resulted in the release of half the working capital.

- The company had transformed from top-down 'command and control' to bottom-up self-leadership. The cells demonstrated their ability to act autonomously.

- The presence of Andrew and Julian started to inhibit further progress and they left the building, never to return

- With no top-down leadership, the organisation established its autonomy and came to life as an independent organism.

POWER TO THE EDGE

Chapter 11

Devolving power to individuals

In hierarchical organisations decision-making is concentrated and centralised. This is primarily because the lines of communication mean that only a few people are privy to all the relevant information. A healthy hierarchy will promote people with a track record of keeping promises and making good decisions. By contrast, unhealthy hierarchies will do the opposite. Even when working well, hierarchies have their drawbacks. Organisations become increasingly dependent upon a few key people and as the organisation grows, the burden on these people grows even faster.

Inevitably leaders become overwhelmed and poor decisions and broken promises result. The common solution is to impose a chain of command with its inherent cost and complexity. This management structure will grow faster than the organisation it manages (Parkinson's Law - see chapter 4). There are also the intangible impacts to be considered. People at the 'coal face' become increasingly disengaged when they have little authority and personal impact, feeling like cogs in a machine.

Matt Black Systems pursued an alternative solution. With their traditional approach failing, they devolved decision-making and promise-keeping. Maximum authority was devolved throughout the organisation, increasing the impact of each person. This is reflected in the term 'power to the edge'.

The Recipe system generated a paper trail of decisions made and promises kept. This allowed individual performance to be identified and audited. People were held responsible and accountable and it took a little while for them to live up to the consequences. Matt Black Systems became a great place to work, if you made good decisions and kept your promises.

What was revealed was a wide variance in responsibility and accountability between individuals.

Defining the talent

> "In any field some people are more talented than others. However, it was difficult to define what talents were involved in making decisions and keeping promises. We came to refer to these talents simply as Magic.
>
> Magic included dimensions beyond committing to a goal and following instructions. If it were this simple, then only conformance and compliance

would be sufficient to deliver results. Our records showed that conforming and compliant people achieved little more than survival. Long-term success required change that brought delight to customers, suppliers, employees and investors alike. When digging into the factors of success, we found imagination (different destination, vision or goal) and creativity (exploration, journey and problem solving). The successful people had done something different."

Julian and Andrew wanted to encourage success but found it difficult to pinpoint its key attributes. Each circumstance was unique, as was the contribution that made the difference. Some people could balance being consistent and effective with being creative and innovative when demanded.

Everyone recognised this Magic after it happened, but who had it, and who could deliver it when required, was more difficult to identify. Everyone claimed the capability, but the best predictor was their previous demonstration of Magic.

"Given the opportunity, people with Magic are keen to demonstrate it. They shine when put to the test, even when the task is new to them. Rarely are they shrinking violets.

We changed our recruitment focus from trying to predict who would succeed, to concentrating on the induction processes. We placed people in the measurement and metric regime as quickly as possible. This revealed who revelled in the limelight. Those with Magic quickly differentiated themselves from colleagues struggling to live up to their promises and commitments. This new approach to recruitment delivered results."

Accordingly, new recruits to Matt Black Systems had a different profile. They were not better qualified, nor more experienced nor more ambitious. They were those who could show they kept their promises and commitments. This proved to be the best predictor of future success in the new model.

"Those with Magic were not all the same type, they had different personality profiles. Talent comes in many guises. What was consistent was their ability to deliver results. From this perspective, we could see why it had been so difficult to predict who had Magic, as they came in so many different forms. Magic was not associated with a particular personality type. We ended up with a variety of people each with a unique perspective and unique set of talents to offer. We avoided the drawbacks of a mono-culture (see Ashby's Law below).

This new intake lifted morale and energy within; staff seemed more engaged with each other and with their promises."

Ashby's Law of requisite variety (W Ross Ashby)

Ashby's Law of requisite variety (W Ross Ashby) is a law used in control systems. It declares that for a system to be stable it must be capable of a wider range of responses than the challenges it encounters. This has implications for organisational systems. If they tend towards a mono-culture or become over optimised, they will be more vulnerable to unexpected challenges that they both don't see and can't respond to. Maintaining a diversity of people and approaches within an organisation's ecosystem is essential if the organisation is to be robust and resilient. Traditional organisational models, as they are patched and optimised, are particularly vulnerable to this problem.

Recovering from the fire

Staff with Magic had a dramatic impact on the organisation and were pivotal to its transformation. In one instance it meant survival, when the factory caught fire.

A neighbouring company suffered an arson attack. Smoke from the fire spread and seeped into the Matt Black building, setting off the alarm and calling the fire brigade. When they arrived the brigade broke windows and pumped in water. Eventually they realised the fire was next door. But by then the smoke and water had destroyed much of Matt Black's factory.

In the immediate aftermath of the fire, the team met and Julian took command.

> "We got together to organise our response to the crisis and I started telling people who needed to do what. They smiled and made clear that all this was in hand and my bossiness wasn't welcome. What they needed was someone to deal with the insurance company and manage the details of the claim. They decided that person was me, so that was my job. They took care of everything else.
>
> After two days we gained access to our factory. The team got to work and sorted everything out. We were operating in a makeshift state the following day. Our customers didn't realise what had happened until well after the event. Two years later there was no financial evidence of the fire, so much so that the insurance wouldn't pay our business interruption claim! That's the power of magical people."

Impact on business results

Putting the highs and lows of events aside, day-to-day business performance had improved dramatically. Customers were happier and suppliers more secure. Employees saw increased opportunity and potential for greater income and personal growth. Investors were happy because profitability had increased and risks reduced. There was a new level of business competitiveness.

Improvements didn't stop. They were relentless in every area of operation. Product and process innovation continued. The benchmark productivity measure of 'sales revenue per person per year' improved as the years rolled by. After more than a decade of self-generated improvements, this measure placed the company at the top of its market sector; a remarkable achievement and validation of the bottom-up approach. Power to the edge works, paying off in both the short, and long term.

> *"We had put a huge amount of effort into shaping the environment; the physical structure and the ruleset. It was clear that we had created a 'void' for each individual to express themselves within.*
>
> *We'd removed the structure and constraints of a traditional company, removed the explicit process instructions and removed all the discretionary processes. This left just the mandated ones. There was nothing left, other than those rules that applied from outside the company. The constraints that applied to each virtual company within Matt Black Systems were the statutory, regulatory and contractual ones."*

The 'Fractal' model

Matt Black Systems is a company made up of virtual companies with the same constraints as the statutory company as a whole.

The image of something made from components that are tiny versions of it-self is captured in the concept of a fractal; shapes that exhibit patterns recurring at different scales. The beauty of this approach is that the fine details of their model are driven, not by Julian and Andrew's ideas, nor by employees, but by the rules imposed by statutory, regulatory and contractual obligations. Within the organisation, these rules are not negotiable or avoidable, yet are not imposed by anyone connected to the business. They are just part of the landscape the virtual companies must adapt to.

"In the end the process was one of removing all the unnecessary, wasteful and dysfunctional things from within the organisation. We removed everything and invented absolutely nothing. The remaining boundaries were not of our making and the only job left for us was to assist people in identifying and understanding the external ruleset. It had been a worthy exercise to distinguish compulsory 'Laws of the Land' from the discretionary rules applied within our company."

Freedom within a framework

The above statement makes it sound as if the internal rules of the business were thrown away and improvements just came about. In practice the 'Requirements; Say-Do-Prove' philosophical framework of Matt Black Systems is a well-crafted and bounded model. By reporting on all the records of the Recipe system and auditing the contractual requirements and the organisational model requirements on a monthly basis, discrepancies are detected at an early stage.

Of course, in the spirit of self-leadership, staff are responsible for ensuring that they are audited monthly, the results are shared and discrepancies acted upon. The employees themselves are responsible for monitoring their measures and metrics in pursuit of their goal of 'enhancing prosperity by forming contracts and satisfying them, successfully'.

'Power to the edge' in practice is explained in the words of one employee:

"The complexity of this role is more than just selling something. You have to be an all-rounder, with an entrepreneurial spirit. Finding such a person is not always easy. There is often a fork in the road. You either choose to embrace the challenge and do a lot of learning yourself, or you say this is greater than my capability.

For example; a colleague and I won a significant order. It was based on proving a concept through a qualification process, including environmental testing, making sure it wouldn't fail. That was scary. Modelling something and making it look pretty was in my comfort zone, but validating that it performed was not.

I embarked on a project where I documented equipment capability; writing statements saying it was airworthy. This brought a ton of anxiety when you haven't done it before. All because I didn't want my project to fail. It was rough.

I took ownership of it. It all rested on me. Communication with the customer, the ability to produce the outcome they wanted, the commercial arrangements. It was all me. In another company that would have been done by a multitude of people."

Summary

- For the new structure to work, power had to be devolved. Each employee was responsible for their virtual company, including the stewardship of resources. They were held accountable.

- Using the Recipe system, measures and metrics, individuals making good decisions and keeping promises were identified. This talent became known as Magic.

- Recruitment placed candidates within an induction framework in order to evaluate their performance rather than evaluate their personality.

- Matt Black Systems became a collection of virtual companies, each with the same constraints as the wider statutory company. The virtual companies provided a void where the people within could express themselves.

- The structure of a virtual company was a microcosm of its parent statutory company and in this sense took the form of a fractal.

- Employees had to balance the compromises between the differing contractual parties in their goal to 'enhance prosperity by forming contracts and satisfying them, successfully'

WORKFORCE IMPACTS

Chapter 12

How things were

Like many organisations the existing staff were accustomed to working in a conventional management system, one of 'command and control' and 'conform and comply'. Each member of staff had a highly bounded area of accountability and could justify their behaviours, they 'did their bit'. People were generally unwilling to make commitments beyond attendance or to be held accountable for the wider impact of their work. Phrases like *"I'll try"*, or *"I'll do my best"*, or *"that's above my pay grade"* were commonplace. They passed responsibility (commitments to future outcomes) to others, both up and down the hierarchy. Activities were process-orientated and time-bounded, following the traditional principle that if you control the process then you control the outcome.

Prior to the reforms at Matt Black, the atmosphere in the building was one of repeating fixed behaviours, staying on familiar ground and maintaining the status quo. Change was seen as negative, as threatening product quality and job security. Many people had manoeuvred themselves into positions of indispensability. And yet, the status quo didn't provide contentment. There always seemed something to complain about, sometimes bordering on the adversarial. Staff seemed to be demanding protection from the vagaries and threats of the outside world, but were not willing to respond directly to its demands and expectations. Despite the air of claustrophobia and frustration, staff resisted change because any alternative was seen as a threat.

Whatever the causes of this malaise, it was longstanding and deeply engrained within the culture. Those with contrasting perspectives had long gone, and internal promotion came with keeping in line and not 'rocking the boat'. Obedience, loyalty and dependability were valued more highly than the use of initiative.

Conversations in the workplace revolved around life outside of work, about the weekend's activities, holidays, football and nights out. The mood towards work was a casual disengagement, there was a veneer of amity; enough to get on and to preserve the peace. This social focus was a distraction from the primary purpose of the organisation, rather than contributing towards it. A happy workplace is not necessarily a productive one.

The seeds of change

> "*After so many false dawns, we had achieved initial success at shifting behaviours through our formative overtime experiment. We realised that our systems were having a dramatic impact on behaviours; they were like the rules of the game being played. Thus, our focus turned away from patching our existing model with the tools of Lean, Agile and leadership initiatives to influence hearts and minds. Instead we turned towards reinventing our model.*
>
> *We created manufacturing cells aligned with the original ethos of Lean. Whilst there is nothing wrong with the tools of Lean, they must be applied within a suitable context. The original ethos was to project context and purpose throughout the organisations to bring meaning to activities. This is the element that is lost when Lean is implemented simply to clean up and to remove waste.*"

The use of colocated teams was key to allow the shift of emphasis to workflow and outcomes and away from functions and processes. Teams worked on a product from start to finish with the goal of satisfying specific contracts. This structure demanded increased responsibility and accountability from staff.

> "*On reflection we had uncovered the reasons behind our previous misadventure with the Lean tools. We hadn't woven context and purpose into the structure of that program. We had imagined that motivational leadership, influencing hearts and minds for the wider good of the organisation, would be sufficient to change behaviours. What we learned was that behaviours are primarily driven by the circumstances surrounding people, both the physical structure and rules within an organisational model.*
>
> *There is no point in giving staff a motivational talk if the structure of their work gives them no sense of ownership of the outcome.*"

The challenge to overcome was that errors or oversights in one process would show up as a problem in subsequent processes. In the new structure, staff were accountable for all the processes, any delays to delivery, re-work required and the impact on the rest of their schedule. This demanded more forward thinking than the previous structure. Initially staff who preferred the narrowest of horizons found the new arrangements challenging.

Some struggled to predict the consequences of their behaviours, or remain consistent in their behaviours and found it next to impossible to live up to this extra responsibility. Some chose to leave, some struggled on, whilst others took easily to this new structure and were pleased to have more control.

These changes resulted in a 'widening' of the culture. Some people used the language of planning and organisation, whilst others continued to complain. The agreed narrative at group level remained negative, yet, for some, back in their individual cells the language had turned positive and progressive. The cells that demonstrated improved performance were also quieter and more organised, whilst the worst ones remained noisy and fraught. The more positive responses by some individuals were not embraced by the group culture, they remained outliers. Some people became far more proactive, whilst others remained reactive and found it a challenge to consider anything beyond the immediate and obvious.

Picking up the pace of change

> *"The ongoing success accelerated our change program. We were quickly identifying those structures that needed reform and were systematically reinventing the organisation. We transformed the structure of our operations without any emphasis on time management.*
>
> *We provided the rules for a new game. We introduced the internal market, our Recipe system, decentralised the admin and put in place a full monthly quality and accounts audit."*

The new cell structure did away with the old supervisory team and line managers. Some redefined their roles whilst others left. This had a profound impact on the mood amongst the remaining staff. It reaffirmed the job security of the productive roles, but revealed animosity and upset between staff and the ex-managers. Whilst the managers and supervisors had been making organisational and logistical contributions in their old roles, it could now be seen that they also had a negative social and cultural impact. Leaders beget followers. Leadership, whatever its approach, imposes the status of follower onto their subordinates.

As change progressed, temporary staff were recruited into those cells with the greatest backlog of work. These fresh people tended to dilute the negative culture within, more often demonstrating a keenness and engagement that was missing in the existing team.

The deep roots of the old culture were unable to resist the pressures brought about by the new structure. The old behaviours were a poor fit for the new demands, revealing themselves to be at odds with the needs of the company and its customers. For those still pursuing the old behaviours, some protested, some tried to adapt, some disengaged and some left.

There was an increased variance between the staff. The workforce fell into three distinct groups, the leading edge who were relishing their new-found autonomy, the trailing edge who seemed fixed in their old behaviours and those in between who were doing just enough to avoid scrutiny.

There were many excuses for poor performance. For example, "I don't do paperwork". The new structure meant everyone was responsible and accountable for their paperwork, which they could subcontract if they chose. Yet those who didn't do the paperwork were also unwilling to subcontract as they would have to pay for the service. They didn't add enough value to pay both for themselves and the support they needed. This put into sharp relief the differing levels of support demanded. Whilst, in itself, providing support was not an issue, when combined with poor performance some demanded more support than the value they were contributing. The Recipe system produced a paper trail of records, but it was the internal market that provided the price discovery that valued each person's contribution to the organisation.

Those who were struggling to adapt were provided with training and support, but many simply chose to leave for more familiar workplaces. The efforts of training and upskilling paid off for them. Staff who left generally took jobs with better pay and prospects than would have been available to them previously. Along with people leaving, new people arrived. These new people quickly found their place within the three distinct cultural groups; those on the leading edge, those on the trailing edge or somewhere in between. Some tensions emerged. Those on the leading edge wanting less interaction with and dependence upon those who were struggling with accountability and responsibility.

Staff who were irresponsible and unaccountable became 'stranded assets'. They were no longer included in the voluntary transactions of the internal market. In time the culture consolidated around the non-negotiable structural elements of the model, the 'rules of the game'. The demands of the environment prevailed over the intransigence of the old culture. On balance, staff numbers reduced as productivity increased. One new person arrived for every two that left.

Playing the new game

Fast-forwarding to the end of the change program, the organisation had been decentralised through the introduction of an internal market, the integration of the admin and finances to the individual cells, the completion of an all-encompassing Recipe library and each individual acting as a virtual company. Every corner of the original model had been restructured and the essential checks and balances were in place.

The Recipe system generated records for every contract and allowed the performance against the agreed quality, delivery, price and control requirements to be assessed. The Balance Sheet and P&L Account revealed the individual financial performance. Audit reported a high level of compliance and the measures demonstrated a successful organisation. Finally, the 'game' was self-sufficient and sustainable. The change program was complete.

The autonomy of the organisation was such that Julian and Andrew were able to pack up their office and leave the building for good.

> "An interesting aspect of our system is the cross-support within the organisation. Each person operates individually as a virtual company, however operating within teams is in their best interest. To achieve this, they form consortia and internal supply chains to satisfy contracts. These voluntary, self-selected teams have proved themselves to be much more effective than the previous teams we allocated to projects, both in terms of capability and cost effectiveness. The individual virtual companies formed into a self-supporting network.
>
> Every system has its challenges, for us it was dealing with poor performers. We had to create a way that the teams themselves could handle this within their network. At some point, most people will have a bad month or two. We introduced an internal 'loan' system where one employee can make a loan to another who is failing. This is a way that the team can demonstrate support and faith in a struggling colleague within the network. It is also in the best interests of the lenders to offer practical help as well as financial support.
>
> These loans are only short term. Chronic poor performance is usually accompanied by the refusal of their colleagues to offer a loan. This is a sure signal that their colleagues have lost faith in them. In this case, the employee falls into 'Rescue and Recovery'."

With the final version of the structure in place, staff turnover reduced. The community settled into the challenge of adapting to the new fixed structure. Skills widened, deepened and the capacity and effectiveness of each person grew.

Along with this increase in competence came an increase in innovation and disintermediation. The dynamic nature of the internal supply chains became more efficient at maximising capacity and minimising constraints. New equipment was invested in and new processes developed.

The culture still had a diversity, and now each member could demonstrate their value. Just like an external supply chain, this allowed for a great variation in the operations and talents demonstrated. Each earned their place in the organisation by being accountable, responsible and financially viable. The culture shifted to one of genuine comradeship.

Putting Matt Black into a wider context.

In the last 30 years there has been a sea change in the way business is conducted and we can sometimes forget how things were.

In the 1980's product life cycles were longer and more stable, routes to market were established and there was increasing consumer demand, high interest rates and high inflation. However, three quarters of the growth in that decade was in retail and services. Manufacturing was not enjoying such easy times. It came under increasing pressure from foreign imports of technology and vehicles (from the far east) and raw materials like coal (from central Europe).

Tariff barriers were reducing and it was primarily market inertia that held back the sale of imported goods. The high costs of investment and employment made many manufacturing businesses simply consolidate in an effort to reduce costs in their fight against competition. For the manufacturing industry, progress was characterised by decline. For its workers, resisting this downward pressure was essential for job security and the prosperity of their communities. The result was that many unions tried to preserve the status quo and supported increases in employment protection.

The aerospace industry was no exception to this pressure. However, as a conservative sector its fortunes lagged behind those of many others. By the late 1990's the same pressures were being experienced in aerospace as well. By this time the wider economy was changing fast.

The pioneers of the internet found ways to disintermediate supply chains (cut out the middle men). This was primarily focussed on importation and distribution, quickly evolving into logistics, retail and services.

Today, the cost advantages of these new routes to market have overwhelmed traditional supply chains. Manufacturing continues to be under huge pressure whilst being starved of investment. High street retail and many service sectors have been pulled into a similar battle for survival. Consumer demand is plateauing, interest rates are almost zero and inflation is low.

In truth, manufacturing is probably more important now than it has ever been, it is just that most is being done offshore more cheaply. In much the same way, retail is also important. It however is moving from a bricks and mortar presence to online platforms. This is being accompanied by the migration of services (such as banking and insurance) to online provision. There are few aspects of modern life that are untouched by the digital revolution.

The disruption of so many sectors of the economy means that there is a real challenge to the traditional functional and hierarchical business model of the 20th century. In the future, businesses will be just as important as they are today, it's just that they will be new businesses with different structures.

As with all forms of automation, there is the opportunity for leveraging the talents of a few highly skilled individuals to provide them with greater rewards. It is increasingly difficult to make decent returns from a more traditional workforce deployed in repetitive work. The new, and seemingly abundant, opportunities have increased the workplace expectations of everyone; but few workplaces using the traditional model can live up to them. The talented employee of today expects work flexibility, great pay and prospects. Traditional organisations find it difficult to recognise the talented, let alone deliver against their expectations.

The mood within Matt Black is positive and professional. People hold themselves to account for their actions and take responsibility for the promises and commitments they make. There is a willingness to place themselves 'on stage' to demonstrate their talents and skills. Work is seen as an opportunity for self-expression and a source of self-esteem and self-confidence rather than a chore to be endured. Talk revolves around the future: ideas, opportunities, plans and risks both inside and outside of work. There are closer friendships and more cooperation and confidence with each other. Teamwork is more effective, better organised and self-supporting, each member having 'skin in the game'.

Surviving the change

Today, just one member of the original team remains in the organisation. He admits that the environment can be stressful, but at the same time highly rewarding. Financially, he is much better off than he was, and better off than he would be in any other comparable company. He enjoys more freedom and control over his work. But this freedom involves risk, responsibility and accountability. Getting the workflow just right to make money every month is a balancing act.

The focus on monthly results can seem relentless. To take a holiday the individual must plan the time off and keep their operations in order. There is a balance between the demands of work in hand and generating a healthy pipeline of new orders. Ultimately, shifting product generates income, and maintaining the flow of work is key to profitability. It's not an environment for the disorganised.

One staff member says:
"Sometimes it is pressurised because you are dealing with a lot of things at the same time. It can very easily get on top of you. We have all had sleepless nights."

But it's not all bad:
"Despite the problems, and every company has them, here the fact that you can see the problems and everything that's happening, gives you security and sense of ownership and power."

They admit that work-life balance is better than in a conventional job:
"For example, if one of my girls needs to be picked up from school, I don't have to ask permission. I just go. If I need to do some shopping at noon on a Tuesday, I just do it."

The work may be pressured but the financial rewards are worth it:
"When you have a good month, you make a huge profit and you get a huge bonus. You feel this place is incredible. You think you've won the lottery."

Finding the right people

Staff turnover during the change program gave Julian and Andrew a challenge. Could they recruit people capable of filling these new roles or were they expecting an impossible combination of wide-ranging skills and self-motivation? Their challenge was to assess whether potential employees would be motivated by the opportunity or overwhelmed by the responsibility.

They tried psychometric tests and found them unhelpful. The data showed that people were adapting to their working environment but it gave no indications of their ability to take on responsibility and be productive. It just proved that major acclimatisation would be necessary if they joined Matt Black Systems. The company needed people who had no expectations of heavily bounded roles. The answer was to recruit new graduates who arrived without the 'baggage' of experience in conventional companies.

"As our cell structure spread, we needed multiskilled people, or at least people capable of being multiskilled. We stopped hiring experts and started hiring graduates, but at similar wages. The graduates quickly showed themselves to be high performers. They were not expert at anything, but pretty good at everything. Our specialists had been held back by their weaknesses, whilst graduates were twice as good at those weak things and quickly became good enough at the specialist skills. This doubled their overall performance meaning their pay rose accordingly.

This is like sports. Playing sport with friends, the winner is whoever has the best overall game. At club level, the winner tends to be someone with a killer move (like a great serve in tennis). It is their expertise that sets them apart. But at national level, everyone has a killer serve, a killer backhand and a killer forehand. Then it is the player's weakness that makes them lose, not their strength that makes them win.

This clearly was what we experienced in our team; we needed great all-rounders. Graduates had a much broader range of ability. They could also trade between themselves when they identified any particular high-level expertise they didn't have. This was a far more productive approach and it didn't cost more."

Summary

- Existing staff were adapted to the traditional organisational model and stuck in a malaise.

- Reform was achieved by staff being swept along by the changes to the physical structure and ruleset of the workplace.

- Some people embraced these changes whilst others stayed firmly rooted in the past.

- The culture widened as a result of the varied responses by individuals.

- As improvements gathered pace, those who didn't suit the new structures searched for new opportunities more suited to their skills.

- The final culture settled and was much more positive and professional.

- Few of the original staff survived the whole journey. The remaining staff enjoyed the benefits and rewards of the new organisational model.

FROM TRAFFIC LIGHTS TO ROUNDABOUTS

Chapter 13

Management Styles

Theory X and Theory Y, as explained by Douglas McGregor, describes two styles of management, one authoritarian (X) and the other participative (Y). How managers view the workforce will largely determine which management style is chosen. Each style requires a different approach by the managers and different structures to support them. These differing approaches can be broadly related to traffic management schemes. Traffic lights with their authoritarian and prescriptive approach are like the theory X management, whilst roundabouts with their focus on cooperation and self-determination are more aligned with theory Y.

Roundabouts versus traffic lights

To explain how Matt Black Systems works, Andrew and Julian take their normal approach of looking at the big picture, the philosophical overview and then introduce the detail picture, the practical methods and techniques. The big picture allows the detailed methods and techniques to be put into their proper context.

First the big picture. If we compare traffic lights with roundabouts, Matt Black operates like a roundabout. Conventional organisations use managers that tell people what to do, like traffic lights instruct drivers. Drivers know they should stop at a red light and green means go. They understand the system imposes order and disobeying is an offence. Likewise, employees know to follow their managers' instructions otherwise they will be disciplined.

Roundabouts, by contrast, have a set of rules that motorists understand. They aren't told when to stop or go, they decide for themselves. They look for a space on the roundabout to enter and move to their exit. Traffic lights use prescriptive control driven by the logical algorithms of their central computer system. It is easy to determine the source of the control. For roundabouts, the 'controlling mind' is far less easy to identify. Leadership and followership are fluidly exchanged amongst the drivers as they use the roundabout. It is a subtle form of distributed control that provides many benefits.

Roundabouts have lower operating costs, fewer accidents and transmit 30% more traffic than an equivalent junction controlled by lights. Interestingly, driver behaviour reveals a lot about their character. Some are creative and safely push boundaries, some simply follow the rules. Others will take big risks and find the rules difficult to follow. Some are too timid, whilst others too aggressive. Some are just plain thoughtless.

There is an imbedded structure and ruleset which is essential to the proper functioning of a roundabout. Matt Black has a particular structure and set of rules, just like a roundabout. It is the detail of the structure and rules that Julian and Andrew think of when they talk about the practical methods and techniques.

Through the structures and rules of Matt Black there is alignment between the interests of the business and its staff. This is achieved through the virtual company approach with its combination of Recipe library and individual measures, metrics, financial reports and monthly quality and accounts audit. The detail of the structure and rules make up the rules of a game that the staff can be left to play.

People are left to make decisions in their own best interests whilst coordinating with their colleagues. They realise the consequences of good or bad decisions and use their judgement within the organisational model. They also know that leadership is not fixed by seniority, but changes depending upon circumstances and competences. The focus on the circumstances of the moment and competences significantly improves the quality of decision-making. This system also removes the need for management. It is more responsive whilst its costs are significantly lower.

Responsible Autonomy

> *"Sometimes the operating model of an organisation is clear and explicit, sometimes obscure and hidden. But all organisations have an operating model, even if they don't acknowledge it. Having an appropriate model is key to success and sustainability. Often, people are so familiar with the model used in their organisation that they take its features for granted; they might even believe their model to be the only possible way. Models may rest on assumptions considered to be self-evident, yet in reality are a choice. They represent articles of faith that are held dear even when they have stopped delivering.*
>
> *This was true at Matt Black Systems. It took time for us to distinguish we had a model and establish that other options were available. In our exploration we identified three fundamental principles that organisational models rest upon; hierarchy, heterarchy and responsible autonomy."*

Hierarchy is a command and control approach in which information is passed upwards through formal lines of communication. The opportunity to make good decisions is only available where the lines of communication converge and the necessary information is available. The decisions flow back down through a chain of command to the relevant subordinates who carry out the commands and whose role is to conform and comply.

In such systems, individuals are ranked and rewarded according to their relative status or authority in the chain of command. The management and administrators are the stewards of the organisation's resources and activities. Such a system is based on the assumption that a limited group of people know best and they should be in a position to exercise direction and control.

Heterarchy is a more representative approach and does not revolve around a chain of command. By contrast with hierarchies, heterarchies attempt to be more inclusive by accounting for the views of as many as possible. They could be considered as a form of crowd sourcing of information and decisions.

Information passes along lines of communication and decision-making is accomplished via discussion and debate; the aim being to achieve some consensus around a situation and proposed actions. Heterarchies are more democratic. Actions are carried out by community members in accordance with the consensus. The more unanimous the consensus, the more effective the outcome. The larger the community, the more difficult it is to generate consensus, most notably in specialist matters. It is essential for the proper function of a heterarchy that a majority of its members have a comprehensive understanding of the issues involved otherwise discussions may be dominated by personalities with little relevant knowledge or information.

Responsible Autonomy is a bottom-up representative system. Individuals make decisions that reflect their circumstances and personal goals and interests. People are in charge of themselves. They can draw upon the opinion of others and enrol them in coordinated activities. Compromises are agreed between individuals. People who don't agree are free not to participate. It is a system based on a set of rules and within these rules people are free to act under their own volition and enter voluntary agreements. People are not free to break the rules; sanctions exist to enforce boundaries.

Our wider communities, such as towns and cities, operate using this Responsible Autonomy model. It is what we are really referring to when we talk about the freedom of individual citizens. Of course, there are rules to obey (laws) otherwise our relationships with fellow citizens would be strained.

Command and control, conformance and compliance, consensus building and community participation are replaced by individual responsibility, autonomy and accountability. In such systems people are free to pursue their choice of creative endeavour within the widest prescribed boundaries. This is a common organisational approach found in small social groups, in large cities and in whole countries. One person is not in charge, nor is a vote taken on every decision.

> *"Each of these organisational approaches has inherent strengths, weaknesses and costs. None represent a perfect model. Real-world models tend to be a combination of them all. The practical outcome is that organisations can only be classified by their predominant approach.*

> *At the start of the journey, we operated a hierarchical model and were failing customers, suppliers, employees and investors alike. The emphasis of our new business model was on Responsible Autonomy. We adopted this model so that each individual could objectively demonstrate the value they brought to the organisation. We felt it could provide the solution to our difficulties and would encourage greater engagement. Responsible Autonomy requires practical solutions for devolving responsibility, autonomy and accountability to the edge of the organisation."*

Responsibility to the edge

The hierarchical approach had concentrated responsibility within management, supervision and administration. The rest of the organisation simply followed instructions. The two principles used to devolve responsibility from the top to the edge were:
- shifting the emphasis from process to outcome
- shifting the 'internal currency' from time to value

Without introducing these two reforms, responsibility could not be properly or objectively devolved.

Shifting emphasis from process to outcome meant challenging the culture of blind compliance. The gateway review method placed emphasis on the quality of outcome to guide activities. Expectation shifted to demonstrating that work conformed to gateway review requirements rather than to a narrow interpretation of instructions. Supervision was replaced by inspection and audit. Evidence that the gateway review had been satisfied was all that was required for the outcome to carry on its journey through the organisation.

" 'Time is money' was the common refrain in our previous hierarchical model. For the individual this meant that the longer they worked the more they were paid. Opposing this, managers and supervisors were responsible for getting the maximum productive work out of the staff. There was a conflict of interests between the workforce and the supervisors. If supervisors prevailed and staff were more productive, fewer hours were worked and either less money earned or fewer staff employed. For Responsible Autonomy to be effective, this misalignment had to be resolved."

The practical solution was a system to track financial incomings and outgoings for each individual, to determine whether their work was profitable. This was coupled with the Recipe library and gateway review records that showed that all contract requirements were met (quality, delivery, price and control). This paved the way for a reward system unconnected to time; one that rewarded behaviours that were aligned to the interests of the business.

This change substituted compliance and hours worked with quality of outcome and a measure of the value-added by the work. Aligning the interests of the workforce with those of the business means that their creativity is directed towards providing tangible benefits. In the long term, higher productivity comes not from working harder, but from making work easier.

Autonomy to the edge

The two practical elements Andrew and Julian used to provide autonomy to the edge were:
- moving from controlling activities to stewarding resources
- moving from following instructions to forming and satisfying contracts

To meaningfully promote autonomy means giving up centralised control over:
- resources (money, machines, materials....)
- activities (sales, design, production...)
- arrangements (meta-models, models, outcomes...)

This does not mean losing track of these elements, but requires alternative systems to achieve the same ends.

The ultimate goal of an organisation is to form and satisfy contracts successfully. This requirement must be devolved to the individuals within. To achieve this practically, each individual must agree to the commitments made in the contracts they undertake and be explicitly responsible for satisfying them. If the commitments, resources, activities or arrangements are imposed by others, then autonomy will be compromised and only a fraction of the benefit will be derived.

> *"The resources being deployed belong to the organisation, so, for autonomy to be achieved, each individual must become the keeper, or steward, of the resources under their control. For us, these resources are simply identified on an individual's financial Balance Sheet. The individual is the steward of the assets on their Balance Sheet and therefore they control their means of production. The financial imperative of this model is that they must provide an income for themselves, plus a surplus in return for the use of the resources. They must form contracts and make commitments, they must arrange their resources and activities such that they deliver on their commitments, satisfy their contracts and create a surplus".*

This high-level imperative provides the freedom for an autonomous worker to seek out work that suits them and be in control of the risks they take. The practical system boundaries prevent the individual from consuming their capital as a salary. Contracts are not imposed on individuals, but the system demands they form contracts and satisfy them in order to prosper from their talents.

An internal free market provides a rich network of customer and supplier contracts in addition to the external contracts that an individual is free to negotiate directly. This network of voluntary contracts is essential for autonomy and to provide the connectivity for individuals within a sustainable community. It is the same system that is used by the wider community outside of Matt Black Systems.

The division of external contracts within the internal marketplace means individuals can specialise. However, they must offer good value to their colleagues otherwise they lose out to external suppliers. Likewise, if an individual dislikes internal offers, they can seek external customers and suppliers.

Every contract includes promises made and terms and conditions to satisfy. The contracts that are chosen reflect the talents and personal goals of the individual. Autonomy can only be achieved when the interests of individuals align with the interests of the organisation. Only then can people be left to strive to get the best for themselves and choose how to achieve it.

Accountability to the edge

With Responsible Autonomy as the organisational approach, a practical way to hold individuals to account was needed. The two main elements used to provide accountability to the edge were:

- moving from process metrics to contract metrics
- changing from top-down contract measures to bottom-up contract measures

With contract metrics of quality, delivery, price and control, the proper satisfaction of contracts could be objectively assessed. The customer doesn't care about the processes undertaken, just that their needs are satisfied.

With the traditional use of top-down contract measures, the contribution of an individual is lost within the complexity, and it becomes impossible to hold individuals to account (other than the ultimate leader). Using a bottom-up approach, the contribution of each individual is isolated and identified as their contract measures are aggregated. Thus, the point of success (or failure) can be clearly identified.

> *"In our old organisation, being 'on plan' was a key attribute. Management and supervision kept operations compliant. Non-compliance was usually categorised as process failure, not individual failure, as individuals were 'just following instructions'.*

> *For devolution of accountability to take place we required an objective assessment of promises kept. We introduced formal contracts for internal and external transactions as a practical solution to this problem. The Terms and Conditions of contract allowed for the objective assessment of promises kept. The initial promises on each contract are summarised by four contract properties; quality, delivery, price and control. 'Control' is key for us as it provides a paper trail of records that forms the basis of our objective evidence.*

> *After a contract is completed, the records show how well the individual has honoured their promises. This holds individuals to account for their promises, supporting the move from process metrics to contract metrics."*

A business can be viewed as a 'money making machine', which is in some sense true. Without profits businesses are not sustainable. Nevertheless, such a perspective fails to capture the complex nature of a business. Beyond survival, a company can't simply exist to make money, there must be a greater goal that drives people.

For Andrew and Julian, it is much more powerful to view a business as a 'social institution'; one with purpose and culture. Their virtual company approach connects business performance to the purpose and behaviour of the individual. Individuals pursue their purpose through the choice of contracts they form. The success of their virtual company allows the sustainable pursuit of their individual purpose.

> *"Success of the virtual company is a reflection of the vision and values of individual operators. Making the most of their opportunities promotes growth in job security, in salary, in self-confidence and employability.*
>
> *The pursuit of individual purpose is at the heart of our organisation. The purpose of our organisation emerges from the aggregation of the purposes of the individuals within. It's a bottom-up approach, where our single corporate purpose is an emergent property, beyond simple aggregation."*

Financial rewards

As well as having an effective auditing system, the new organisation also has a unique financial reward system. In the traditional business model employees are rewarded for time. They are paid by the hour or by the day, so the more time they spend at work the more money they get. What they do in their work time is largely down to the employer. Unsurprisingly, people tend to work long hours and have low productivity. There is no link between the pay of the employee and their productivity or the success of the business. Essentially it is up to the employer to make the employee productive in the time that they pay for.

The challenge for Julian and Andrew was to create a reward system that both balanced the needs of all parties and encouraged beneficial behaviours. A simple "if you do this, I'll give you that" carrot and stick approach would be insufficient. After many iterations, an approach was devised in which the lion's share goes to the employees.

The employee's basic salary was derived from two elements. One was the 'statutory minimum wage', based on their contracted hours of work, as demanded by employment law. In addition, a further multiple of the statutory minimum wage is provided based on a person's 'employment disposition'.

The employment disposition was evaluated based a person's predisposition towards Recipes:
- Pre-follower – can follow a Recipe, with oversight, and meet requirements
- Follower – can follow a Recipe, without any form of supervision, and meet requirements
- Changer – is a Follower who can also change a Recipe to meet additional requirements
- Creator – is a Changer who can also create a Recipe to meet new requirements

The above is an oversimplification of the employment disposition model developed by Andrew and Julian, but it is the essence of their model. As it turned out this model proved to be a very useful tool in distinguishing the predisposition of their staff towards their Recipes.

The combination of the two elements above make up the basic salary package for an individual. It is market leading because of the multiples derived from the person's employment disposition. For example a 'Changer' may receive up to four times the statutory minimum wage as their basic pay.

In addition, there is also a success bonus based on sharing the profit as follows:
- 20% for the employee to take home as part of their monthly salary
- 20% goes into an investment account at the discretion of the individual employee
- 20% goes into an investment account to be used for the organisation as a whole
- 20% provides return to the investors
- 20% goes to the Tax authorities (simple corporation tax)

The two types of investment account controlled by the employees form an important element of the profit sharing scheme. These are influential in revitalising the means of production as well as providing the opportunity to explore alternatives. This underpins the autonomy of the individual and fosters an entrepreneurial spirit that would otherwise be absent.

In aggregate this recasts the social bargain. It is not uncommon for an employee to double their salary via the success bonus. The primary rewards go to the employee and the community. To the employee via their basic salary and success bonus, and to the community via Corporation Tax on profits, VAT on sales, National Insurance, Payroll taxes as well as other Local Authority taxes. The investors get interest on their investment as well as a 20%

share of the gains. The power of this model is that it is transparent as to how everybody gains, this is in direct contrast to the traditional hierarchical organisational model.

Summary

- Matt Black Systems moved from a 'traffic light' system to the 'roundabout' approach of 'Responsible Autonomy'

- Responsibility was devolved to the edge of the organisation by moving the focus from process to outcome and from time to value.

- Autonomy was devolved to the edge of the organisation by moving the focus from controlling activities to stewarding resources and from following instructions to forming and satisfying contracts.

- Accountability was devolved to the edge of the organisation by the move from process metrics to contract metrics and from top-down measures to bottom-up measures.

- The social bargain of the organisation was recast to both improve and better share its rewards.

PAYOFFS DELIVERED

Chapter 14

Payoffs from the changes

The journey had been a bumpy one. In hindsight, Julian and Andrew can now reflect on the business benefits of the new model as well as the advantages for investors, customers, suppliers, employees and to the wider society.

Business benefits

Dividing the organisation's Profit & Loss account across every individual resulted in an increase in profitability. As is often said, "whatever is measured, improves". The traditional centralised P&L is too remote from the workforce to actually influence their behaviours. Making this connection is one role of management and supervisors.

Most organisations rely on an internal currency of time, around which their operations are ordered. The translation of contract requirements into the time-bounded internal activities is an expensive overhead. The activities enter a logistical plan that must be managed and monitored, this is another role of managers and supervisors. Seldom do things go to plan, and with such a time-bounded plan any delay will require the remaining plan to be recalculated. Very rarely are these delays resolved so that the plans are brought back onto their original timeline.

Relinquishing time as the internal currency and substituting financial constraints and contract terms had many impacts. Firstly, management and supervision were no longer needed as translators. Secondly, there was a new-found flexibility within operations. Because the operators are in charge of the plan, they can change it as circumstances dictate (see Bayes' Theorem –Chapter 7).

The simple internal trade system allowed each person to freely enrol their colleagues in their projects as well as participating in the contracts of others. Finally, the financial literacy of the staff increased enormously. This didn't mean that everyone was focussed solely on making money, but rather that their decisions were at least bounded by financial constraints.

> *"We observed a change in behaviour in the product assembly area. Previously, at the end of a shift there would be a few parts scattered on the floor, parts that had been inadvertently dropped during the processes. The operator had reached for another part rather than picking up the dropped one. In time, the floor was free of these dropped parts and even the amount of general waste materials reduced as people were more frugal with their supplies."*

Through many small changes the organisation became more effective at generating profit, without people needing to work harder. This made the organisation more sustainable. The introduction of individual Balance Sheets and a charge for the capital deployed made a significant reduction in the total resources under stewardship. Within a relatively short period, the organisation released more than half of its working capital, significantly increasing liquidity.

Matt Black Systems now boasts a larger order book, reduced risks, fewer problems, more profit, less waste, less working capital, more agility, better staff engagement and greater liquidity.

> *"One measure we regularly review is yearly sales revenue per employee. Previously this was a lamentable £57,000, about three times our median wage. Today, this has increased by a factor of five and is still growing. The pay of our staff has grown by the same proportion. We have transformed from a low wage employer to one paying premium wages. By the measure of yearly sales per employee, our organisation has moved from near the bottom to near the top of our industry.*
>
> *This huge productivity increase was not the result of any one change. It was the cumulative impact of many innovations in product, service and process across all activities. It is tempting to imagine that success comes from a single solution. The search for a 'magic bullet' to resolve all ills, is wishful thinking. The pursuit of such a singular solution is a distraction from the important work of encouraging the hundreds of small changes that aggregate to deliver real success."*

Traditionally structured organisations typically fall into crisis when they are overwhelmed by legions of small problems. Their centralised mechanisms become saturated with information to be assessed, decisions to be made and actions to be carried out. Their systems don't have the 'bandwidth' to cope with the volume of corrective traffic. The tendency is to focus on just the urgent problems and leave more trivial things unaddressed. These trivial issues grow into the urgent problems of the future, fuelling an unending cycle of problems. In hindsight, this was the case for Matt Black. The situation only improved after Julian and Andrew identified that the organisation's mechanism to resolve its problems, its immune system, was compromised. Their centralised system was failing. Decentralisation transformed this immune system and the organisation was able to 'self-heal'.

"Perhaps the most substantial benefits were the intangible ones. Whilst these were not directly measurable, they were observable. For us, work no longer seemed a burden. This was demonstrated by the enthusiasm with which we sprung out of bed on Monday mornings. No longer did we feel we were pushing the organisation along. It had a life of its own and was pulling us. That was evident in every interaction. Truly, the culture had changed."

Investor benefits

The shareholders, Andrew and Julian, felt more secure in their investment. The capital tied up in operations has reduced as the organisation does more, with less. Profitability has grown as has retained earnings. Together this provides more opportunities and less risk.

"There is a better return on our investment as well as more security. For us, the journey has produced more than financial reward. We have freedom to step away from the business and our day-to-day role. Our lifestyle has improved and become sustainable. We both have more time to spend with our respective families."

Their roles as Directors and as Investors have been separated. They no longer have an office in the building. They grow their investment portfolio with other projects. They find new opportunities to apply their model and make long-term investments.

Customer benefits

Customer distress was the primary motivator for change. Customers were demanding that the business meet its contractual promises of quality product, delivered on time and in full, at the agreed price whilst meeting the wider control standards required by the industry. This was not an unreasonable expectation.

The transition to a new organisational model was challenging for customers and every effort was made to reduce the impact they felt. It took a while for the new organisational model to gain critical mass before customers perceived any improvements. But then improvements came swiftly. The backlog of contracts disappeared, deliveries were on time and customer returns plummeted. Later, lead times on new projects halved.

The essential customer contract metrics have significantly improved:

- Quality: from 'unknown' (some deliveries were returned for re-work but not properly reported), to better than 99% of contracts where no items were returned under warranty or complaints received.
- Delivery: from 17% to >98% of deliveries made on time and in full to contract.
- Price: from 'unknown' (invoicing mistakes were not formally recorded), to 100% where the price promised to the customer was the same as the invoice sent.
- Control: from 'unknown' (based on a sporadic audit providing only occasional snapshots of compliance) to >98% of contracts known to be compliant (as proved by thorough monthly audit of the Recipe records).

> *"Whilst our performance is not perfect, consider the nature of the business sector. Matt Black Systems is not an intermediary or aggregator, where quality is a reflection of putting the right thing in the box despatched. We produce aerospace equipment, and design and develop entirely new equipment that undergoes rigorous type testing. These high-level metrics cover all types of work and reflect how remarkably little of the prototype equipment fails during testing. Achieving this performance, within this context, is a remarkable turnaround."*

Supplier benefits

Initially the new contract metrics applied to suppliers put them under additional pressure. Non-conforming product was quickly returned, as expectations were clearly defined and anything not up to standard was rejected. This high level of scrutiny identified many more problems than previously. Some suppliers even criticised the spotlight they were under. By contrast, other suppliers found a benefit from being in direct contact with the cells using their products and the feedback provided. It took a little time for suppliers to become comfortable negotiating with the cells rather than with the central purchasing specialists they had previously built a relationship with.

The new relationships with suppliers came to be based upon contract performance and not amity. Internal and external suppliers were treated equally and loyalty to them was based explicitly on contract performance. Good suppliers, with good contract metrics, benefited from increased business and improved communications.

As Matt Black Systems transformed from a reactive to a proactive organisation, the requirements upon suppliers became more organised and predictable. The rigour of the quality, delivery, price and control metrics meant suppliers who fell short would eventually be deselected. Given the way Matt Black's customers had persevered with them, even when the performance was poor, Julian and Andrew chose to provide their suppliers with the same opportunity to work through their problems. Only the ones that could not improve their performance over time eventually had their relationship terminated.

Employee benefits

Perhaps the most significant gains have been for employees. Their employment contracts formalised a significant change to the bargain between staff and the organisation. Their time wasn't sold for a fixed price. They were selling their talents and had a stake in the success of the company. Both their influence and their rewards grew. This was a material shift in the social contract with the staff. Money is not a prime motivator, but too little money is certainly a demotivator. The new structures provided ways for the employees to influence their rewards to meet their individual circumstances.

Individuals set their salaries within a pay framework. This framework does not reference the 'hourly market rate' for the job, but the value the individual generates through their activities. Pay is not connected to the hours of attendance and there are no 'clocking-in' systems to track hours worked. As with any contract, the employment contract contains promises and commitments. Some will over-promise and fail to deliver. The measures and metrics provide all the evidence required.

The pay structure allows an individual to return to the pay framework as often as they are able to generate the evidence for a pay increase. People can fast track their basic pay, mirroring their increased ability to utilise their talents and add value. In some cases, this new approach led employees to earn double or even triple what they could command in the wider employment market.

> *"Previously we had low pay and low productivity. Our pay rates were suppressed to the lower levels for our market. This contrasts with today, where our basic pay and entitlements are above the industry average. In addition to improved basic pay, each employee also receives two fifths of their individual monthly profit.*

Each month, one fifth of their profit goes to them as part of their remuneration. This bonus can add significantly to their income. It is not unusual for it to add a further 100% to their already high basic pay, taking their package far above the industry norms.

The other fifth passes onto their individual Balance Sheet for investment purposes. The individual is the sole steward of this liquid asset. Our aim is to nurture the entrepreneurial talents of our people not only their productivity. Many people have tens of thousands of pounds accrued in their investment accounts; company money that they are the sole steward of."

In the new organisational model, employees are in charge of their basic pay but it is directly linked to their talents and the tangible contribution they can demonstrate. The thoughtful individual will claim the highest basic salary they feel comfortable committing to, without over-promising in relation to their future success.

The people of Matt Black value their intangible benefits such as freedom and autonomy. Individuals make real impactful decisions with regard to their work which gives them a strong sense of self-determination. They feel like the authors of their work, rather than the followers of it.

"Success is well rewarded and is a reflection of the talents and skills that are put to work. There is a strong culture of mastery. They convey a strong impression of self-confidence and self-esteem, derived from their professionalism. It was noticeable after a few years that individuals walked taller, became more direct in their communications and were happier to showcase their talents and skills.

The self-leadership required by the system poses an existential question; what direction to choose?

With freedom of choice comes the burden of decision-making. Some revel in this autonomy, whilst others find anxiety in the freedom.

In one sense the direction of travel is simply a matter of self-expression in the moment, but for most this demands a more purposeful reflection. Their choice of work today will impact their near future and will help define their long-term. Choosing a direction that provides the life they want, becomes the force that shapes their day-to-day decisions."

This self-direction has become one of the most valued parts of working in the new model.

Benefits to wider society

Organisations exist within a wider society and cannot be separated from it. What happens within businesses will impact the community around them. High quality, well paid jobs must be the goal rather than lots of low skill, low paid jobs. Many businesses are marginal, corners are cut and wider requirements are ignored in response to immediate concerns. In the long term the community around them suffers.

Matt Black Systems is a fit, healthy and compliant organisation with an effective 'immune system' and provides secure employment. The local community benefits beyond local tax revenue when it contains secure and successful companies. When jobs are well paid, long-term and open to the people of the community, the benefits are enjoyed most widely.

Summary

- The changes made to the organisational model benefited the business, its customers, suppliers, investors, employees and the wider community.

- For the business, the changes delivered a larger order book, reduced risks, fewer problems, more profit, less waste, less working capital, more agility, better staff engagement and greater liquidity.

- Customers benefitted from the removal of the work backlog and lead times halved. Quality, delivery, price and control were transformed.

- The demands upon suppliers became more organised and predictable as Matt Black Systems changed from a reactive organisation in crisis to a well ordered and proactive one.

- For investors, higher profitability and lower risk meant a better return on their investment as well as more security of their investment.

- Employees benefit from a new social contract emphasising the value they add rather than the time spent at work. Success results in well paid, secure jobs, with an unprecedented degree of opportunity and self-direction.

- The wider community benefits from secure and well-paid jobs open to talented local people. The stability and wealth provided encourages further investment within the local community.

500%

Chapter 15

A quick recap

In the introduction to this book we told the story of Pete and Joe the window makers. As their business grew, productivity (windows per person) had halved. In the end, they were half as productive by this measure as they had been when Pete and Joe worked on their own. Before the reform, Matt Black had followed the same path with much the same results. The conventional wisdom, of further specialisation made the situation worse as it grew staff numbers and increased the challenge of coordination. This is a common problem in Europe and the US, the knowledge industries being more sensitive to the drawbacks of the division of labour.

Julian and Andrew took up the challenge that faced Pete and Joe; how to remedy the loss of productivity that had occurred as they scaled. For Julian and Andrew, this meant decentralising and converting from a top-down organisation to an organisation driven from the bottom-up.

Matt Black had a huge backlog of work and it was struggling to remain competitive. These issues were the focus of the turnaround project in this book. But in all the change something unexpected happened, something extraordinary. Productivity increased by more than 500%.

This is such a significant change, one that has transformed the future of the company, and one that is of particular significance as companies in Europe and the US struggle to gain even the smallest productivity improvement. The productivity revolution at Matt Black Systems is worthy of further assessment and review.

Defining productivity

> *"At MBS, we don't just look at the number of widgets made per hour as a measure of productivity, we take the value of the widgets sold, divided by the number of people in the whole workforce. We use this measure because it integrates all the labour that must be covered by the sales revenue rather than just the direct labour.*
>
> *Thus, we use a simple proxy for productivity; sales-per-person-per-year. In our system this measure is built from the bottom-up, so we start with sales per individual per year and then aggregate them for the business as a whole. By using an internal market, the value of the internal services can be included.*

We started this program with our productivity averaging around £57,000 of external sales revenue per person per year. Today, by the same measure, our productivity averages greater than £300,000 and amazingly is still climbing. Some of our virtual companies are significantly higher than even this sum."

On the ground, the number of employees has dropped from twenty five to six and the total sales revenue has increased by a third. The 500% increase in sales revenue per employee is an aggregated number for the business as a whole. Digging down into the details of each virtual company shows subtle differences in how this increase in productivity was achieved. Transformation has not come through one particular route but is made up of several 'stand out' ingredients.

In summary, productivity gains were driven by the combination of six key factors:
1. Redesign of admin
2. Reduction in errors
3. Waste Reduction
4. Overcoming constraints
5. Facing the customer
6. Alignment

Redesign of admin

In the decades before the reforms, the admin and management systems built up, layer upon layer, in response to problems or new demands. There had been little design effort at integrating these new parts, each simply added to the burden. The systems had not been so much designed, as congealed, never benefitting from holistic review.

The Recipe system provided the basic building blocks for both the operational and administrative activities. The addition of the 'virtual companies' provided the context needed to ensure that these Recipes both worked together and were manageable for a single person. This holistic review was essential to streamline the Recipes with the target that ALL the admin should take no more than 20% of a person's time (one day per week).

Time and again, the redesign removed multiple steps from admin tasks and connected parts that were previously handled by different functions. For example, it is a small extra burden for the goods inward inspection (that verifies goods received as conforming to requirements) to approve the payment to the supplier. This significantly simplified the admin of supplier payments. Previously, the Quality and Accounts functions shared this activity between them, and this required coordination.

The benefits of the system redesign were large, in some cases admin costs were reduced by 90%. For example, the overhead cost of getting a part ordered, delivered, stored, kitted and supplied to the line fell from £26 to £2.50. In general, it is estimated that the redesign of the admin and management system reduced its costs by 75% (this was mainly labour).

The impact of the changes to admin and management were profound and far reaching. Initially about a third of the staff were engaged in various forms of admin and management. These included supervision, quality management, stores, finance and accounting, human resource management and purchasing, as well as a range of bureaucratic activities associated with statutory and regulatory compliance. These people were paid more and were responsible for nearly half of the payroll costs. In addition, they added a burden of their own to the overheads such as office space, IT and HR admin.

> "We had started with a rather simplistic intent to cut these overhead costs by devolving the admin and management to the productive workforce. They were paid less so it seemed to make sense to get the lowest paid people to do these activities. Initially, we saw this as a simple task transfer with its associated cost saving. But, as it transpired, so much of the admin was being double and triple handled (data was raised by the productive staff who passed it through various other hands before being completed) that the savings were dramatic."

Reduction in errors

Previously the business had been dogged by a multitude of small errors and oversights that subsequently became very disruptive and time consuming to resolve. The variation between people was not so much in the speed at which they worked but the consistency of their work. Some people were inconsistent and created a myriad of small, almost undetectable, problems. Problems that were later revealed in different functions and required significant amounts of rework.

The reforms revealed that these problems were being generated by only a small number of people. Testing and tracing these errors back to source brought about behaviour or staff change. The number of small problems and oversights dropped significantly. Operations and admin were able to proceed more smoothly and speedily.

The multiskilled approach, where staff carry out most of the operations on a single product or service, meant that any problem created in the early part of a process would inevitably return as a burden at some later time. There was no payoff to turning a blind eye to problems. Consequently, staff tended to make sure things were done properly before they used the parts in subsequent processes. Staff now saw each step of their work in the context of the entire production process; they became proactive and not just reactive.

Staff were much more engaged in their work, partly because they had such a direct impact on their work-life.

Initially, the new-found engagement saw a flurry of changes to tooling, processes and logistics as the problems encountered were resolved rather than ignored. In time, production work became much more ordered, calm and predictable.

Waste reduction

Initially, the tools of Lean provided very little improvement to productivity; their implementation often being more costly than the savings made. However, as the change program progressed and waste was removed from the operations, the specific reforms used by the individuals in the cells often came to resemble the Lean approach. Perhaps the changes were introduced in a different order than before. For example, surplus stock was consumed and operator movement within the cell was reduced rather than the standard consultant led approach of first tiding up using the '5S' tool (see chapter 4).

> *"Wherever opportunities for improvements were found, individuals motivated by the new organisational model and its reward system, drove waste out of their processes. This applied equally to operational and administrative activities. This removal of waste reduced cycle times by as much as 50%"*

Many of the changes to plant and processes required considerable investment. This is where the individual investment accounts held by the virtual companies came into play. Each individual had their own retained earnings to reinvest in improvement projects. If successful, they provided increased funds to replenish their investment account as well as enhancing their personal prosperity. This approach saw a flurry of successful investments in plant, product and processes and further reductions in waste.

With the multiskilling approach and reduction in waste, workflow became significantly smoother. The multiskilled operator is automatically able to start the next process having completed the previous one.

Before the reforms, parts were moved station to station, entering a queue in each and waiting for the specialist operator to become available. With a multiskilled operator, the products don't need to move much and there is no queuing involved; both product and operator are constantly engaged. Once started, the products flow seamlessly to completion. This improved flow significantly reduces the work-in-progress as well as the burden of logistics and coordination. Improvements are not driven by working faster or harder but rather by people striving to make their work easier and enhancing their individual prosperity.

This improvement in flow has been especially noticeable in the reduction of lead time: the time between the initiation and satisfaction of a contract. The undivided attention of a single operator who makes an explicit promise to a customer has had a dramatic impact on the timeliness of deliveries. Lead times have halved, as has the product development cycle.

These changes have provided a better service to customers, more pressure on competitors and an increase in productivity through greater sales revenue.

Overcoming constraints

In the operations at Matt Black, with low volumes and frequent changes in product mix, constraints and capacity limitations are difficult to both identify and address. This is not because they are hidden, but rather because they move around constantly in response to the particular circumstances of the day. For example, with lots of small projects on the go, a queue of work appears in the design department and they became a backlog. With complex projects that contain thousands of components, the backlog moved to purchasing as they struggled to source all the components quickly.

Initially a solution based on constraint theory was pursued but quickly it became obvious that it had little impact on the overall capacity. The internal market had been introduced as a means to establish the value that each person was contributing. However, it also provided other benefits, one of which was its ability to quickly and effectively redirect workflow around constraints, even the ones that moved about.

The internal market relentlessly sought out any pockets of under-utilised capacity when its normal routes became congested. As products came and went and as demands varied, capacity utilisation has become both consistent and maintained at a high level.

Facing the customer

As the operators became increasingly multiskilled, they eventually came to embrace the sales function too. This meant processing new orders for repeat contracts and negotiating contracts for entirely new products. As the very same operator would be designing, scheduling, manufacturing and delivering, it is in their best interests to negotiate terms that they are comfortable they can satisfy. They are acutely mindful of contract risks. Simultaneously they consider the design challenge, their workload, stock levels, supply chain capability, tools, equipment and the profit they want to achieve. This joined-up thinking helps to de-risk projects from the start. It sounds a lot for an operator to cope with, but in reality, it uses the same skills needed to plan a dinner party for which they have to shop, cook and deliver to the table.

The previous specialised sales team would all too often over-promise and agree to demands that the rest of the organisation would find difficult to satisfy. This inevitably resulted in increased costs and customer distress.

Alignment

The original overtime system at Matt Black did not serve the organisation well, it rewarded counterproductive behaviours. The redesigned measures, metrics and reward system specifically focussed on aligning the interests of the individual, the organisation and the customer. In serving their own best interests, individuals served the interests of others in a win-win relationship.

> *"Striving for success is fine as a concept, but to bring it about in reality the measures of success must be aligned, objective, transparent and their feedback immediate. We made a brave decision, early on in our change program, to share as much information as appropriate. In some cases, the culture had to gain a degree of maturity before the information shared could be usefully*

interpreted. Information transparency had to be introduced at the rate that people could understand and integrate it."

The feedback provided by the measures and metrics was key in identifying beneficial behaviours which allowed people to shape their activities accordingly. The transparency of information between the virtual companies meant that benchmarking could also take place. Each person could compare their results, their successes and failures with those of others to look for new ways to further improve.

Bringing the parts together

It is difficult to assess the importance of any one of the factors above, as none stood out from the others. Indeed, even as individual factors they were not as significant as they became when combined into a single holistic system. The total being greater than the sum of the parts. It is the combination of all these improvements, as well as the myriad of minor improvements that has transformed, and continues to transform productivity at Matt Black Systems.

As each of these elements were introduced, and leveraged off the previous introductions, the productivity at Matt Black started to climb. It climbed more than Julian and Andrew had ever imagined it could. At each stage they believed they had reached the limit of what was possible. But with the introduction of the next stage in their program, productivity would climb rapidly again. Astonishingly, the overall improvement in productivity has been greater than 500% and still continues to rise.

The improvements in productivity have not come at the expense of performance in satisfying contracts. The number of items returned under warranty has dropped to less than 1%. Less than 2% of deliveries miss the promised date and quantity. Invoices now match the agreed contract price. Less than 2% of contracts are not compliant to the wider statutory and regulatory control requirements.

Summary

- Matt Black systems adopted a simple measure of sales revenue per person per year to monitor their productivity.

- The redesign of the admin processes and their integration into the cells significantly reduced costs.

- Removing the source of the huge number of small errors had a dramatic impact on disruption.

- The new organisational model encouraged staff to reduce waste in admin and operations to improve workflow.

- The introduction of the internal market had many benefits, one being that it was very effective at overcoming the moving constraints within the operation.

- Multiskilled people were able to strike better compromises throughout their activities. This was especially evident when sales activities were devolved.

- The new system aligned the interests of the individual with the organisation and its customers.

- Combined in a holistic system, these individual factors supported and amplified each other. The overall improvement in productivity was greater than 500%.

LESSONS LEARNT

Chapter 16

The fractal model

The fractal model has proved itself at Matt Black. Andrew and Julian have since applied it elsewhere, with equal transformational impact. They are spreading their investments and decreasing their dependence on the aerospace industry. They look for opportunities in organisations with high labour content and with local costs and competition.

What is stopping its wider adoption? The benefits for business owners, employees and customers are clear. But it is difficult for business owners to justify such a root and branch transformation. The biggest resistance, however, comes from existing management teams who perceive such reforms as threatening. They would rather try another patch to their old model.

Maybe organisations need a crisis to jolt them into action. That was the case for Matt Black. It was a failing company, forcing Julian and Andrew to challenge their fundamental assumptions and question the very basis of their model and its ability to deliver. They took a highly analytical view of work design and concluded that genuine and fundamental change was necessary. They chose to decentralise, to pass much of the control to the people doing the work; power to the edge.

From their analysis, it was clear that the conditions necessary for traditional, 'command and control' models were becoming more challenging and were going to get worse in the future. Margins were low, investment returns poor and cheap compliant labour with the necessary skills was no longer readily available. Nevertheless, the data revealed that parts of their organisation were highly effective, and this drove the focus of their exploration.

The answer to their problems was not in addressing the symptoms of failure. They had tried Lean, Agile and new Leadership approaches that influenced hearts and minds, but none made any sustainable difference. The answer lay in the underlying disease. Once they reformed their organisational model, they were rewarded with sustainable change and success. Their new model enabled the organisation to first heal and then grow.

> *"It's the Model stupid! Our old model was keeping us sick. Just patching its symptoms meant we never really got better. It isn't just us who are suffering, many organisations are realising that their circumstances have changed for good and they need to move with the times. A new model is required. For new businesses this is much easier, there are lots of start-ups exploring new*

models, but a single successful model for the twenty first century hasn't yet emerged. We are still in the exploration phase.

The question for us was: could we survive until an alternative model became popular or must we devise one for ourselves? For other organisations facing this same challenge, the answer depends on the willingness and capability of senior management to explore, design and implement a completely new organisational model. A tall order for most."

In spite of their determined efforts, the resolution of their productivity problems didn't come from improvements and optimisation of their old model. It resulted from the transformation to a new one. The key skill in this transformation was design, not leadership. With the introduction of their new model, everyone would become a leader and no one would be subjugated and limited to the role of follower. This placed new demands upon the staff but also dramatically increased their engagement.

Mimicking supply chains

The structural change that had the greatest impact on behaviour was the creation of an internal market so that people traded with one another using formal and voluntary agreements. This allowed everyone to value the work that everyone else did; a form of internal price discovery. For this market to work it had to be free of central control and manipulation yet needed robust checks and balances to minimise distortions.

"We explored voluntary trade in a pilot scheme first. The dispatch department tracked the value of goods they sent to customers and kept the amount they felt they needed to pay for their time and ingredients. They passed what was left upstream to their productive colleagues who did likewise for their suppliers.

This exploration worked well. Each person was quite good at estimating the market value of what they provided. The internal distribution of the money was successful until the fixed costs were added and apportioned to each function. It was then we encountered a problem. When these invisible, although essential costs were added there was not enough money available to reach back to the suppliers. The team struggled with the fact that a large proportion of their budget was needed to cover fixed costs; most of it being administrative labour."

The experiment was revealing. It identified that jobs worked best if they passed through the fewest hands. This gave momentum to start multiskilling. This reduced the number of hands all jobs passed through. The more tasks each individual did, the larger the proportion of the value of the job they could retain. However, the biggest gain was achieved when individuals took on more admin and management duties; this had the most impact on their costs.

The new multiskilled approach, where jobs passed through the fewest hands, exposed a general skill shortage in some of the existing staff. They were used to managers taking responsibility whilst they narrowed their attention to their familiar tasks. For some, expanding their skills and taking on simple administrative tasks was unpalatable. They wanted someone else to be responsible and eventually left the company for jobs that suited them better.

There are plenty of self-employed people successfully running their own businesses. Some of them collaborate in professional or personal networks in order to tackle larger pieces of work. Generally, this is how a supply chain works. Supply chains distribute and devolve the responsibility for the end product throughout. No organisation is responsible for everything. Even the last organisation in the chain, the one that produces the finished goods, will only be responsible for the final stage.

This is the mechanism that Matt Black Systems adopted internally. Each person exists within a rich internal market and participates in many supply chains. This approach has proved to be more effective at optimising the capacity of the organisation as the mix of products and demands change. Not just limited to simple production issues, it also encompasses the changing admin and management burden. With all eyes on the circumstances, the organisation is more attentive to change as it occurs and can respond effectively to maintain efficiency.

The contracts that link the people in the supply chain hold each party to account for their outcomes and responsible for their commitments. A Profit & Loss and Balance Sheet for each employee is a critical requirement and the ultimate arbiter of individual sustainability. This financial autonomy is a prerequisite for the achievement of personal autonomy and self-leadership.

In the wider world, supply chains are capable of delivering large and complex outcomes. The essential feature of real-world supply chains is that they require no central control. They are not perfect, but they avoid intensive information flows and have lower managerial and administrative costs; the savings are especially great during times of rapid change and reorganisation.

Supply chains also work for all sizes of business.

The application of the supply chain approach within an organisation, provides distributed or bottom-up control. It is a real alternative to central control and management. Today, this approach is more attractive than ever because information technology has reduced the costs of automating administration. This is why we have seen a recent proliferation of organisations exploiting distributed control. Information technology is the game changer, it has provided the gateway to alternative organisational models.

Bottom-up versus top-down

The 'supply chain' model is bottom-up, whereas the 'command and control' model is top-down. Beyond an organisation of just a few people, the top-down model means that those with influence are increasingly only those at the top.

For those not in control, their influence on the organisation becomes minimal and insignificant. Whilst the traditional model has its advantages, the costs and inflexibility of plans, budgets, centralised information flow, decision-making and the disengagement of employees make it a poor fit in today's world where these aspects make the difference between success and failure.

By contrast the bottom-up approach means that autonomy and influence is preserved throughout the organisation. The devolved Profit & Loss accounts and Balance Sheets become a reflection of the impact that individuals have upon their particular circumstances. When an employee can clearly see and benefit from their contribution, engagement follows.

> "We faced an organisation that had firmly hit against these top-down limitations in a declining market. We were forced to explore alternative models that could revitalise our business. We moved towards a low cost, flexible and decentralised approach, arranging our employees in a network of single person cells.
>
> We were determined to devolve as much accountability and responsibility as possible to this community of individuals. We had observed time and again that, as organisations grow, they became less efficient (see Ringelmann Effect below). Inefficiencies accelerate over time and come to a head if the organisation stops growing or their market enters a downturn.

We reasoned that this was the result of people losing touch with the context of their tasks, and yet this is something that is not so apparent in supply chains."

The traditional organisational model seems to provide benefits to growth and yet increases the penalties when growth ceases. This is largely due to the fact that as traditional organisations expand, their roles divide into narrower specialities (of which their staff have existing knowledge). However, when they are forced into contraction they have the additional problem that their staff need to broaden their skills as they take on additional roles (of which their specialist staff have limited experience).

The Ringelmann Effect

The tendency for individuals to be less effective as the size of their group increases. Max Ringelmann noted that as the number of members of a tug of war team increased the average force applied per person decreased.

Teams are not more effective than the sum of the individual capabilities. Being part of a team can encourage motivational loss and social loafing.

Differing approaches

As individuals, Andrew and Julian looked at their organisation through different lenses.

Andrew as a wide innovative thinker, looked at the system as a whole and took responsibility for the design of the organisational model. He is by nature a synthesist: he has an exceptional ability to see and form patterns.

Julian as a deep, procedural thinker, focused on the practical details and taking the responsibility for the human side of the organisation. Julian is by nature an analyst: he has an exceptional ability to distinguish and structure detail.

Together they took a scientific approach to the problem of matching the world of humanities with its psychology, anthropology and sociology to the world of business structures with its sole traders, larger corporations and marketplaces. Only through experimenting, observing the effects and analysing the results were these separate disciplines combined to deliver a sustainable organisational model fit for the humans it accommodates.

"Both of us respected the other's viewpoint and were prepared to listen. We accepted that we had our own biases and were willing to challenge each other, without falling out. Time and again our individual thinking had proved to be wrong, we had fallen prey to our individual blind spots and inclinations. Together we were able to identify our blind spots and so prevent us wasting time on bad ideas.

In hindsight, this initially led to a rather uncomfortable time when we both undermined each other's ideas leaving us a little adrift with no solutions. We didn't fall out over this, but rather entered a period of exploration together. We started with a clean sheet of paper and designed the organisational model from both a systemic and procedural perspective. We repeated a cycle of synthesis and analysis, forcing ourselves out of our respective comfort zones. Both the big picture and the detail picture are essential. The 'devil' is not to be found just in the detail!

We viewed the traditional organisational model as best at accommodating a narrow range of people. For everyone else it is an uncomfortable fit. Over time, and invisibly, the organisational immune system rejects people who don't fit in. You are left with people who are either disengaged or those who lie in this narrow range and who largely think the same."

The turnaround challenge

If this experiment had been a new company, it may have run more quickly and smoothly. But Andrew and Julian had an existing organisation and employees steeped in a traditional way of working. They not only had to establish a new and viable model (just like any new organisation must), but they also had to take their established model and transition it to the new one. This has the added time and cost of retraining, of breaking old habits and expectations, establishing new contracts and agreements and resisting the temptation to go back to old ways.

Ensuring that each step on the journey remains functional and effective adds costs and delay to a slow transition. It would be cheaper, quicker and less stressful to establish a new model in a new organisation, or even pilot the new model alongside, but separate from, an existing organisation. At least there would be no costs and difficulties associated with transitioning an existing model. The pilot method is the one that Andrew and Julian have chosen in their investments elsewhere.

Something to look out for

Bottom-up systems have to be carefully designed with a firm eye on their emergent characteristics.

> *"The easiest problems to deal with are those that appear immediately and directly from their cause. You make a decision and it is proved to be right or wrong. We can adapt and refine our systems quickly to this sort of problem. However, there is a category of problem that is delayed in its appearance and is only indirectly related to the decisions made. Immediate and obvious vs delayed and obscure. The latter types are far more difficult to adapt to.*
>
> *There is a further category to be wary of: those artefacts that are not simply the deterministic reaction of a system but ones that appear as a result of system-wide interactions and feedback. These are 'emergent properties', artefacts that have to be detected and observed rather than determined and predicted. For example, the cultural appetite for risk and willingness to engage in risky activities is not something that can be predicted or determined. The appetite for risk waxes and wanes, the result of complex feedback between group members. There are so many influences on risk-taking that detection and observation are essential if behaviours are to remain sustainable throughout the transition."*

The direction of an organisation is another emergent property, given by the individual direction of each of its members. There are many examples of organisations with declared purposes that are in conflict with the actual purpose that can be implied from its visible activities.

Devolved, self-leading organisations are also uniquely vulnerable to dominance by personality. There is an adage 'never let a crisis go to waste'. There are always those who aim to garner control and influence. During times of duress they lobby for authority over others or their resources. Often these controlling types subtly change the rules of the system to reward discipline and compliance. Presented as an advantage to all, responsibility soon 'flows' uphill, a hierarchy starts to grow and the inevitable reversion to 'command and control' is baked in.

> *"The pursuit of individual purpose must be guarded as a pillar of the organisational model. Failure to maintain a network structure will inevitably result in a controlling hierarchy. Individuals who are overwhelmed by the pressures of accountability and responsibility find it easy to take one step back and let others shoulder their burden. The opposite is also true. Controlling types are eager to assert their dominance. Checks and balances are necessary to prevent hierarchy from returning."*

The future

Would Andrew and Julian do it again?

> *"Undoubtedly, we learned a huge amount from the experience. We have applied these insights elsewhere to great success and benefit. However, the journey was long and painful at times. Our project took us ten years. We stumbled in the dark, making mistakes, learning and painfully 'unlearning' as we went. If we had known what we know now, things would have been easier and quicker. We progressed carefully into the unknown, every step was made without destabilising the organisation. Every step either produced an improvement directly or was a step necessary to get to our next improvement.*
>
> *It partly explains this book. We want to communicate our experience and provide a new tool. We want to show that transformation from a top-down, product focussed organisation to a bottom-up, customer focussed organisation can be achieved and that there are even a few shortcuts available."*

Most leaders facing a financial crisis do the opposite of empowering their people. They cut costs and pull power back to the centre. They rely upon controlling and directing their business, which means telling people what to do. They waste enormous amounts of energy dealing with the crisis of the moment, without seeing it as a symptom of a deeper issue. They shuffle people around in a 'reorganisation' and make a few redundancies but never confront the redesign that their organisation so desperately needs.

And why should they? Decentralisation means they are likely to end up reducing their power and importance. If they can tweak the current model, satisfy the short-term needs of the shareholders and maintain their personal status, that's what they will do.

In a competitive marketplace, organisations that increase productivity by 500% cannot be ignored. The experience of Matt Black Systems shows there is a viable alternative waiting to be adopted. It needs bold and insightful people to make it happen. Leaders able to let go of personal power, design an effective model and devolve their power into that model. Mavericks determined to challenge conventional thinking about organisational design. People resolute and visionary like Andrew and Julian. It seems such people are rare.

INDEX

123

5S 51, 144
5Whys...51

A

acceptance check............................... 80
accountability 37, 103, 111, 112, 114
.... 117, 124, 127, 154, 157
Accountancy Principles.................... 95
accounts 58, 76, 79, 81, 113, 122
activities 80, 82, 93, 95, 112,
.... 123, 124, 125, 126, 134,
.... 137, 142, 147
admin 41, 47, 79, 80, 81,
.... 96, 113, 115, 153
    costs.. 143
    framework.................................... 80
    processes 74
    project 79
    Recipes 79, 82
    system 76, 79, 142
    tasks..76
    team.................... 46, 49, 63, 66, 81
administration activities 75
    system 76
administrative costs 49, 153
aerospace................. 13, 19, 71, 74, 136
aggregate 129
Agile 19, 112, 151
agility 134
Airbus 9
aircraft................................19, 22
aircraft designer.......................22, 56
alignment...............................28, 146
analysis...156
anxiety 107, 138
arrangements................... 125, 126
artefacts................................157
Ashby, W Ross.............................. 105
Ashby's Law 104, 105

attendance 111
audit ... 80, 81, 82, 85, 86, 87, 89, 113,
122, 124, 136
auditing system 128
authority 103, 123, 157
autonomy................ 47, 57, 61, 82, 95,
.... 99, 100, 114, 115, 124,
.... 125, 126, 130, 138, 153, 154

B

Backlog.................... 22, 27, 28, 32, 47,
............................51, 52, 66, 67, 72,
............................113, 135, 141, 145
backlog bonus 48, 51, 66
Balance Sheet 96, 98, 115, 126, 134,
................................138, 153, 154
barriers 21, 44, 47, 79
basic pay 89, 129, 137, 138
basic salary 128, 129, 138
Bayes Theorem 72, 133
Bayes, Rev Thomas 72
behaviour 39, 42, 47, 63, 83,
.... 97, 111, 112, 114, 128,
.... 133, 144, 146, 147, 152
benchmarking...............................147
benefits...50, 139
best interests 122, 146
best practice................................ 86
big picture...............81, 93, 95, 96, 97,
....121, 156
blame.. 37
blind eye 144
board of directors........................... 56
bonus....................47, 48, 51, 52, 58,
.... 67, 96, 97, 118, 129, 138
bottlenecks............................27, 31, 64
bottom-up................99, 123, 127, 128,
.... 141, 154
boundaries............... 20, 57, 93, 94, 95,
.... 97, 107, 123, 124

budget 96, 152, 154
bureaucracy 45, 78
business benefits 133
    books 24
    interruption 105
    model 24, 39, 128
    owners 151
    performance 128
    process 30
Buurtzorg 13

C

capability 99, 104, 107, 115, 146, 152
capacity 32, 95, 116, 145, 146, 153
capital 52, 98, 126, 134, 135
capital equipment 64
cash flow 52, 57
cell capacity 85
    division 90, 94
    finances 67
    metrics 96
    profitability 85
    structure 113
    teams 41, 63, 81, 85
central admin 82
    control 152, 153, 154
    store 41, 49
centralised admin 50
    control 125
    functions 49
    teams 49
chain of command 103, 123
change management 30
change model 22
changer 129
checks and balances 52, 93, 95,
.... 115, 152
circumstances 112, 123, 137, 153
Clyde 46
Cobham plc 15

colocated teams 51, 112
comfort zones 21
command and control 42, 111, 122,
.... 124, 151, 154, 157
commitments 85, 126
community 124, 139
company law 79
Company's Act 95
competence 21, 116
compliance 55, 71, 74, 75, 79,
.... 82, 83, 94, 103, 115,
.... 124, 125, 136, 143, 157
conflict 45, 46
conform and comply 111, 123
conformance 63, 71, 73, 74, 82,
.... 94, 103, 124
consensus 123, 124
constraint theory 27, 145
consultants 19, 28, 29, 30, 31,
.... 32, 37, 85, 144
context 14, 112, 121, 136, 144, 154
continuous improvement ... 82, 87, 99
contract 75, 98, 115, 125, 126,
.... 127, 136, 137, 145, 146
    law 79
    metrics 52, 67, 94, 127, 136
    performance 136
    price 147
    properties 52, 127
    requirements 133
    review 80
    terms 133
contracted hours 40, 128
contribution 154
control 21, 47, 48, 51, 58,
.... 63, 64, 98, 111, 113,
.... 115, 117, 123, 125, 126,
.... 127, 135, 136, 137, 147,
.... 151, 154
control systems 105

corporation tax...................................129
cost-plus.. 58
costs.........................38, 45, 46, 47, 48,
...............................50, 56, 57, 58, 59,
...............................60, 61, 66, 74, 75,
...........................80, 82, 122, 146, 151,
....153, 154
counter-incentives............................ 39
creativity.................................104, 125
creator..129
crowd sourcing..................................123
culture....................38, 63, 66, 83, 111,
....................113, 114, 116, 124, 128,
.................................135, 138, 146
customer benefits............................ 135
  contract..............................51, 87, 88
customers.................19, 22, 28, 29, 30,
.... 31, 47, 51, 64, 71,
..............85, 89, 126, 135, 146, 151

D

debtors.. 38, 58
decentralisation.......51, 52, 53, 57, 62,
....79, 86, 134
decentralised admin.........................113
  approach..............................85, 154
  model....................................55, 57
  operation.....................................50
decision-making........ 47, 99, 103, 122,
.... 123, 138, 154
declaration of intent.........................75
delivery.................... 19, 22, 40, 49, 50,
.........................51, 58, 112, 115, 125,
.... 127, 136, 137
demarcation...................................... 46
departments........................... 45, 55, 56
de-risk.. 146
design.....................15, 23, 56, 75, 80,
.............................125, 145, 146, 152
  approach.. 22

brief..80
limits... 23
review 80
devolution process............................64
directors............................... 56, 79, 95
disciplinary process.......................... 89
disease............................33, 37, 38, 151
disengagement.........................111, 154
division of labour.....................81, 141
document control system.................76
documented process..........................72
double handling.............................. 58

E

economies of scale...................... 14, 52
ecosystem..................................100, 105
emergent property 128, 157
employability 128
employee benefits............................137
employees............. 13, 27, 30, 104, 107,
...................118, 128, 137, 138, 142,
.... 151, 154, 156
employment contract...30, 87, 88, 89,
....97, 137
  disposition........................... 128, 129
  law.. 79, 128
engaged 16, 29, 42, 94, 95,
...........................104, 143, 144, 145
engagement 51, 66, 71, 93, 94,
...........................113, 124, 134, 144,
....152, 154
entrepreneurial behaviours............. 98
  spirit 107, 129
ethical... 96
evidence..................... 75, 124, 127, 137
excuses..37, 114
experiment..............36, 39, 40, 41, 48,
.... 72, 73, 76, 86, 153, 156

F

Far East 46
feedback 49, 72, 100, 136, 146,
.... 147, 157
fiduciary duties 79
final test 75, 80
financial constraints 133
    crisis 87, 158
    imperative 126
    measures 52, 96
    performance 60
    reward 47, 128, 135
    transactions 60
fire 105
fixed costs 66, 67, 152
flexibility 50, 56, 133
Flight Refuelling 15
flow 19, 21, 28, 118, 145
follower 113, 129, 152
fractal 106, 151
framework 107
free market 126
freedom 82, 97, 117, 123, 126,
.... 135, 138
functional barriers 21
functions 57
Future Work Forum 13

G

game 40, 112, 113, 114, 115,
.... 117, 119, 122
gateway reviews 73, 74, 75, 76, 79,
.... 81, 82, 85, 88, 124, 125
glue syringes 52
goals 19
Gore, W L 13
governance 76, 81
graduates 119

H

habits 41, 74, 83, 86, 156
head count 45
Health & Safety 75
hearts and minds ... 30, 31, 38, 112, 151
Henley Business School 13
heterarchy 122, 123
hierarchical model 124, 125, 130
    organisation 45, 103
    structure 21
hierarchy 21, 61, 80, 103, 111,
.... 122, 157
holistic 19, 22, 28, 79, 80,
.... 81, 142, 147
Holm, Andrew 13, 15
hours 39, 40, 125, 137
HR 79, 81, 95, 143

I

imagination 33, 104
immune system 28, 38, 63, 134,
.... 139, 156
impact 20, 31, 39, 97, 103,
.... 112, 113, 134, 135, 144
improvement 24, 27, 29, 37, 66,
.... 86, 87, 90, 94, 144, 147
incentive 51, 66
income 89, 98, 106, 118, 126, 138
induction 104
influence 21, 23, 39, 81, 137, 154
information ... 103, 122, 123, 134, 146,
.... 147, 153, 154
information technology 56, 154
innovation 72, 106, 116
insight 23, 33, 96, 97
inspection 19, 20, 73, 74, 76,
.... 80, 81, 85, 124, 143
instructions 71, 72, 73, 76, 83,
.... 88, 103, 121, 124,
.... 125, 127

insurance 66, 105
integration 64, 75, 115
internal market 54, 57, 60, 65, 67,
.................87, 89, 93, 113, 114, 115,
.... 141, 145, 146, 152, 153
inventory.......................................41, 49
investment......... 29, 86, 88, 129, 135,
....138, 144
account......................129, 138, 144
investors...........................129, 133, 135
invisible manager 38, 40, 42
invoice 57, 58, 136

J

James Wilson (Engravers)
Limited..15
Japanese..51
job security 31, 38, 97, 111, 113, 128

L

labour content..................................151
  costs...................................46, 67
law 30, 45, 75, 95, 107
layout...28, 29
lead time..................................135, 145
leader................. 23, 103, 127, 152, 158
leadership ... 112, 113, 121, 122, 151, 152
leading edge 51, 67, 85, 114
Lean.............................19, 20, 28, 29, 30,
..............................32, 38, 41, 47, 51,
.... 71, 72, 85, 112, 144, 151
legacy....................................63, 80, 83
limitations....................22, 23, 75, 154
line-balancing.............................. 28
liquidity 134
loan... 38, 115
logic 31, 42, 46
logistics 27, 49, 144, 145
long hours 128
loopholes.. 93
losses.. 87

low productivity 27, 128, 137
loyalty...111, 136

M

Magic 103, 104, 105
management........... 37, 38, 39, 40, 47,
..........................56, 71, 81, 83, 111,
..................121, 122, 123, 124, 133,
..........................142, 143, 151, 154
manipulation 21, 152
margins 151
market 93
market rate..............................137
mastery.............................. 138
Matt Black Systems....................15, 19
McGregor, Douglas.....................121
measures 19, 22, 32, 38, 42,
...........................48, 85, 96, 97, 99,
.... 107, 115, 122, 137, 146, 147
meltdown...19
Meta-recipe 76
meta-models...................................125
metaphor............................. 28
metrics............. 32, 52, 96, 97, 99, 107,
............122, 127, 136, 137, 146, 147
micro-management.................. 83, 88
miscommunication 21
misdirection 65, 93
mistakes......................21, 93, 99, 136
model...................... 24, 39, 46, 47, 56,
.... 80, 93, 94, 95, 107, 112,
.... 114, 115, 122, 126, 152
money............31, 51, 86, 117, 125, 128,
.... 137, 138, 152
mono-culture 104, 105
morale 104
Morning Star 13
multiskilled 21, 42, 46, 47, 49,
...............................64, 87, 119, 144,
......................................145, 146, 153

N

National Health Service 60
needs 81, 127, 128
negotiation 50, 66
network 40, 86, 115, 126, 154, 157
no-blame culture 16
non-compliance 94, 127

O

obligation 89, 95
observation 72, 157
office space 143
online retail 56
on time and in full 22
operator 88, 89, 94, 145
opportunities 63, 86, 93, 95, 97,
.... 117, 128, 129, 135, 151
optimisation 23, 24, 28, 152
optimism 28
order book 87, 134
orders 49, 118, 146
organisation 16, 23, 38, 41, 45,
.... 46, 56, 83, 99, 112, 113,
.... 114, 115, 117, 128, 158
organisational change 22
    design 55, 56
    model 63, 94, 122, 135, 138,
    .... 144, 151, 154, 155, 156
organism 100
OTIF 22
outcomes 73, 112, 124, 125, 153
outgoings 125
output 29, 39, 40
overhead functions 61
overheads 60, 61, 80, 143
over-invested 98
over-promise 137, 146
oversight 71, 88, 129
overtime 31, 38, 39, 40, 42,
.... 47, 89, 112, 146

ownership 37, 41, 48, 97, 112, 118

P

P&L 60, 66, 67, 96, 115,
.... 133, 153, 154
paint spraying 20
paper trail 79
Parkinson, Cyril 45
Parkinson's Law 45, 103
pay 39, 40, 89, 97, 98,
.... 119, 128, 134, 137
payoffs 133
payroll costs 143
performance 37, 38, 40, 49, 52,
.... 66, 82, 87, 88, 94,
.... 95, 99, 103, 106, 113,
.... 115, 119, 136, 137, 147
personality 100, 104, 157
Pete and Joe 13, 14, 141
philosophy 74
pilot 22, 23, 56, 81, 82,
.... 85, 97, 152, 156
pipeline 118
planning 72, 75, 81, 113
poor performance . 37, 85, 87, 94, 114,
.... 115
power to the edge 103, 106, 107, 151
pre-follower 129
price 50, 51, 52, 59, 114,
.... 115, 125, 127, 135, 136, 137
proactive 99, 113, 137, 144
probability 72
problem 21, 37, 38, 46, 71,
.... 89, 94, 97, 104, 112, 144
process 31, 47, 71, 72, 73,
.... 74, 75, 85, 88, 112,
.... 124, 127, 134, 145
    control 71, 73
    improvements 73, 85
procurement 48, 49, 51, 57

product design 75
mix 145
production 20, 21, 29, 40, 72,
........................75, 80, 85, 125, 129,
....144, 153
production manager............ 49, 64, 65
productivity...............13, 14, 16, 19, 21,
............................27, 28, 31, 32, 38,
............................39, 40, 42, 46, 47,
............................50, 51, 66, 82, 85,
.... 89, 93, 97, 106, 114,
.... 125, 128, 134, 138, 141,
...........142, 144, 145, 147, 152, 158
professional 96, 100, 117, 153
profit........................31, 51, 55, 58, 59,
............................85, 96, 97, 98, 118,
............127, 129, 134, 137, 138, 146
share 129
profitability 67, 85, 86, 89, 93,
.... 97, 106, 118, 133, 135
project management.........................15
promise-keeping 103
prosperity..........................96, 107, 145
psychology......................................155
psychometric tests...........................118
purchasing............. 48, 49, 50, 52, 80,
...................................136, 143, 145
purpose.................................... 128, 157

Q
quality.................... 16, 19, 20, 40, 47,
.... 49, 51, 71, 72, 73,
...............................74, 76, 79, 81, 82,
...........................87, 94, 99, 111, 113,
.... 115, 122, 124, 125, 127,
.... 135, 136, 137, 139, 143
quality control 71, 74
queuing...145

R
Recipe.......76, 79, 81, 82, 93, 129, 136
library 81, 95, 96, 115, 122, 125
system 85, 94, 99, 103, 107,
.............................113, 114, 115, 142
redundancies.............................39, 158
regulations............................ 13, 74, 79
regulatory requirements 52, 75, 88,
.............................96, 106, 143, 147
remuneration................................. 138
reorganisation 74, 153, 158
reporting......................................48, 107
requirements 79, 80, 107, 125, 129
Rescue and Recovery..........88, 89, 115
resistance 21, 29, 30, 38, 61,
....74, 81, 151
resources 98, 123, 125, 126, 134
responsibility 20, 37, 47, 48, 58, 87,
.........................93, 95, 103, 111, 112,
.....................113, 114, 117, 118, 124,
......................................153, 154, 157
Responsible Autonomy.........122, 123,
.... 124, 127
retained earnings............. 98, 135, 144
retraining...156
return on investment..................... 135
revenue 37, 40, 51, 55, 58
revenue per person............ 45, 51, 106,
....134, 142
reward system 125, 128, 144, 146
rework..................... 20, 74, 85, 99, 143
Ringelmann Effect 154, 155
Ringelmann, Max 155
risk......... 41, 73, 95, 117, 134, 135, 157
root cause analysis..............................51
roundabout..............................121, 122
ruleset...........40, 42, 86, 106, 107, 122

S

safeguarding..81
salary 96, 126, 128, 129, 137
sales revenue.....................47, 142, 145
savings...............................143, 144, 153
Say-Do-Prove.......................75, 76, 107
schedule 46, 63, 75, 112
scientific approach............................155
Scotland 46
security....................................118, 135
self-determination 121, 138
self-confidence 117, 128, 138
self-direction 138
self-employed 153
self-esteem 51, 97, 117, 138
self-expression 117, 138
self-financing 66
self-improvement.............................. 89
self-leadership 13, 98, 107, 138, 153
self-management 94, 98
self-motivation.................................118
self-reliant... 99
self-selected......................................115
self-serving 56, 74
Semco 13
shareholders 135, 158
shipbuilding...............................46, 47
silo 20, 45, 55, 57, 61
Sisyphus...21
situational analysis........................... 22
skill shortage.....................................153
skills 20, 46, 63, 64, 83,
........................98, 116, 118, 138, 153
social bargain 129
    contract.............................97, 137
society 133, 139
software..60
sole trader 55
South Korea...................................... 46
specialisation..........14, 46, 55, 80, 141

sprayer 20, 21
staff........................ 30, 39, 40, 41, 107,
....................111, 112, 113, 129, 134,
....137, 143
stakeholders...................................... 56
start-ups..151
status 61, 113, 123, 158
status quo 31, 39, 56, 111
statutory company 106
    constraints...........................52, 106
    minimum wage................. 128, 129
    requirements.... 75, 93, 107, 143, 147
    submissions...............................75
stewardship................................98, 134
stock 41, 48, 52, 57, 146
stock control........................48, 49, 50
storemen 41
stores 41, 42, 48, 143
stranded asset............................ 82, 114
stressful............................... 14, 117, 156
structure..................20, 22, 40, 42, 61,
........................94, 106, 112, 113, 114,
...............................116, 119, 122, 157
sub-cells 94
subcontractors................................... 59
sub-functions 45
subordinates............................. 61, 123
success......................16, 19, 81, 85, 87,
........................94, 96, 97, 104, 112,
.....................113, 127, 128, 134, 137,
...............................138, 146, 151, 154
success bonus........................67, 85, 89
success story 16
supplier payments 143
suppliers..................20, 49, 50, 55, 57,
........................58, 60, 63, 66, 75,
...............................126, 136, 137
supply chain 63, 66, 71, 115, 116,
.... 146, 152, 153, 154
surveillance.......................................72

sustainability 122, 153
sweet-spots...21
Switzerland 37
symptoms 19, 31, 33, 65, 66, 151
synthesis 156
system 33, 40, 46, 51, 105,
.... 115, 121, 122, 123, 126,
....139, 143
system map...81

T

talents........................ 89, 103, 104, 116
...............................117, 126, 137, 138
target 40, 41, 142
tax..66, 79, 129
tea 72
teams............................. 30, 31, 94, 115
teamwork 117
templates...76
temporary labour.............................. 32
Theory X 121
Theory Y...121
time 124, 125, 128, 133
   delay 49
   management 113
timesheets.. 46
top-down 127, 141, 154
top-down measures.........................127
traffic lights 121
trailing edge 51, 66, 67, 85, 114
training............32, 38, 86, 87, 88, 114
transaction system 57
transformation................ 151, 152, 158
transition 49, 135, 156, 157
transparency......................................147
turnaround 15, 22, 38, 96, 136,
....141, 156
turnover 116, 118

U

Uuneconomical...................................73
unintended consequences 83
unions 46
upskilling 114

V

validation... 106
value 96, 97, 116, 124, 126,
.... 137, 141, 145, 152
value-added 48, 51, 52, 58, 67, 125
values...128
value-stream 28
variance.................................... 103, 114
virtual company ..95, 96, 98, 99, 106,
.... 115, 122, 128, 142, 144
vision...............................19, 51, 104, 128
void... 106
voluntary agreements.....................152

W

wage.. 134
warranty.................................... 136, 147
waste... 47, 85, 112, 133, 134, 144, 145
Wilson, Julian..................................13
Wimborne 15
window business 13
work design 151
   flow......................20, 27, 28, 49, 55,
..............................112,117, 145, 146
working capital 98, 134
work-in-progress..............................145
work-life.............................89, 118, 144
workspace.. 28
Wright, Orville and Wilbur 23

If you wish to know more:

We have Authored a Book Titled 'Introducing your Invisible Manager' ISBN 9781092913225. It is an abridged version of this book and a 'reader friendly' introduction to the subject of organisation design for self-leadership.

There is also a free resource for people interested in developing their own self-leading organisation:

Fractalwork.com

Author Biographies

Andrew Holm

Andrew is a serial innovator and organisational architect. He is a co-owner and director of Matt Black Systems and is best known for his work on organisational modelling and business transformation. He studied electrical and electronic engineering in Glasgow and was a design engineer within the shipbuilding industry in Scotland. He continued his career within two large multinationals within the spheres of project management, sales and marketing management and finally as a commercial director.

Andrew has completed numerous business turnaround projects and is a recognised thought leader in self-managing and self-leading organisations. His expertise lies in the design of innovative organisational models and making them happen. He is the creator of the first fully integrated software application for self-leading organisations and is the founder of the fractalwork.com website, a free resource for people wishing to take their first steps into this subject. He co-authored the first book on self-leadership based on Matt Black Systems, titled "Introducing Your Invisible Manager", and speaks internationally on the subject.

Peter Thomson

Peter spent the first half of his working life in HR, ending up as the Personnel Director for Digital Equipment in Northern Europe. He then continued to develop his interest in the developing world of work by setting up and running the Future Work Forum at Henley Business School. He also established himself as a consultant, advising organisations on the introduction of new ways of working.

Peter is co-author of the best-selling book "Future Work" and contributor of chapters and articles to numerous other books and magazines. He regularly blogs on the latest developments in work and most recently has focussed on productivity and self-management. He speaks at conferences and other events on the emerging trends in work and their impact on leadership.

Peter is a Director of FutureWork Forum Ltd, a think tank providing inspiration to business leaders worldwide. He also runs Wisework Ltd, a leading consultancy in the field of flexible working and is a member of the steering team for the Reinventing Work Network, run by the RSA.

Julian Wilson

Julian is a multi-disciplinary design engineer (BSc) with a strong interest in the social sciences. He is a co-owner and director of Matt Black Systems. Having spent several decades designing aerospace instruments and their manufacturing processes, the growing challenges of the business moved his focus from working IN the business to working ON the business. Julian's strong interest in the humanities took him to study psychology and qualify as a therapeutic counsellor. Organisations are social institutions and not machines; this training gave him a powerful insight into the life of their organisation rather than just its operations. Armed with years of experience in design innovation, it was natural to approach the challenges of organisational change with the same rigour and eye for the small details. As a business owner who had made the transition from leader to model designer, he has first hand experience of the difficult emotional journey that must be undertaken by any leader who transforms their organisation to self-leadership. He has written academic papers on Knowledge Management and is the co-author of "Introducing Your Invisible Manager". He is a passionate promotor of self-leading organisations and speaks on the subject internationally.

Made in the USA
Monee, IL
10 December 2020